Lorraine Cavanagh is an Anglican  and was Anglican Chaplain to C author of *The Really Useful M* Stoughton, 1995), *By One Spirit: Reconciliation and Renewal in Anglican Life* (Peter Lang, 2009) and *Making Sense of God's Love: Atonement and Redemption* (SPCK, 2011). She translated *He Took Me by the Hand: The Little Sisters of Jesus Following in the Footsteps of Charles de Foucauld* (New City, 1991). Her paintings have been exhibited at the Living Art Gallery, London (1981 and 1984).

FINDING GOD IN OTHER CHRISTIANS

Lorraine Cavanagh

First published in Great Britain in 2012

Society for Promoting Christian Knowledge
36 Causton Street
London SW1P 4ST
www.spckpublishing.co.uk

British Library Cataloguing-in-Publication Data
A catalogue record for this book is available from the British Library

ISBN 978–0–281–06585–1
eBook ISBN 978–0–281–06586–8

Typeset by Graphicraft Ltd, Hong Kong
First printed in Great Britain by Ashford Colour Press
Subsequently digitally printed in Great Britain

Produced on paper from sustainable forests

For the students of Cardiff University chaplaincy,
past and present

All names have been changed and certain details of individuals' experiences altered or modified in order to preserve confidentiality

Contents

———•◆•———

Acknowledgements

———◆·◆·◆———

My thanks go to the following, all of whom have helped to make this book possible: to my husband, Sean, for his patient reading and perceptive comments, and for his support and encouragement; to Christopher Kizza and Miriam Shanti for their stories; to Alison Barr for believing in the book and for all her encouragement and support; to all at SPCK; and to the chaplaincy students who lived out the vision and to whom the book is dedicated.

Introduction

Christians often end up doing the one thing they least expect. In my case, it is writing a book about reconciliation. I am someone who runs a mile the minute there is the slightest rumble of disagreement in the air, especially when it involves other Christians. I would rather contentious topics were quickly resolved, or even avoided. But I have also learned that people who simply don't like arguments have to be very clear about why they want the argument to end, or not to happen at all. Is it a matter of anything for a quiet life? Or is there a real yearning for reconciliation? The two are not the same thing. The quiet life amounts to having as little meaningful exchange with other people as possible. It leads eventually to isolation and loneliness. Genuine reconciliation is about reconnecting with others in a more truthful way because it allows trust to get re-established and builds on what has been learned in the conflict. So Christians have to decide which of these two scenarios they really want.

Writing this book has revealed to me that reconciliation happens when warring factions want it for the right reasons, so if we are going to have disagreements, they ought to be productive. They ought ultimately to be a source of enrichment for all parties. Bland confidence that a state of equilibrium will happen by itself, or that the situation can somehow be managed away without anyone getting hurt, never works. Wanting to resolve disputes out of a desire that peace should prevail at all costs entails further risks. Everything depends on what kind of peace we are looking for. Is it the kind which ignores the realities of injustice or betrayal? This is what Jeremiah accused the false prophets of doing, declaring peace when there was no peace (Jer. 8.11). Or is it the kind of peace which comes with the renewal of friendship or genuine understanding and empathy? This is the kind of peace in which we learn trust, or learn how to recover trust when it has been lost or damaged.

Trust is the ability to be vulnerable, first to God and then to others. It is only really learned through being able to receive love and return it without fear of betrayal. Trusting God and trusting other Christians are two sides of the same coin. We can't learn to trust others if we don't first trust God, and we can't experience what it is to trust God if we are not willing to find ourselves eventually trusting those Christians with whom we think we have nothing in common. Where there is anxiety about other Christians, or about the kind of God we say we believe in, it becomes very hard to establish peace.

Conversations I have had with people in the course of my ministry as an Anglican priest have revealed that the kind of trust which leads to real peace only happens when we *experience* God and his grace. But experiencing God does not guarantee a quiet life. We engage with him with all our human faculties and this can turn our lives upside down, especially with regard to how we relate to other Christians. Experiencing God and his grace also obliges us to experience being the Christian we feel uneasy with, or just dislike, so it entails great personal risk. Experiencing God means wanting reconciliation between Christians in the way we want God himself. John writes, 'Those who say, "I love God", and hate their brothers or sisters, are liars' (1 John 4.20); we can't have it both ways.

John's words have been embedded in my own consciousness ever since I came to adult faith. I have never been able to stop dreaming of reconciliation in the Church, and by Church I mean all those who formally, or informally, call themselves Christians. I have tried telling myself that peace between Christians is unachievable this side of eternity, but somehow the words have a hollow ring to them. This is because they are inherently untrue, as St John says in his letter. If those who claim to follow Christ cannot be reconciled, it implies that Christ's coming to us, and involving himself so intimately with the human predicament, was a wasted effort and that human beings and the Church itself are a waste of God's creative energy and love. While I recognize that there are people who may think like this, and have given up on the Church altogether, I know that every moment of goodwill between Christians, every quarrel resolved, every good or kind action done in defiance of distrust and hatred, is a sign that God's grace is still at work and that he does not view the Church as a wasted effort. For this reason, I also believe that Christians can and must be reconciled if their work of mission and evangelism is to be at all credible, and it is in this spirit that the book came to be written.

I am not suggesting that all Christians should agree and like one another simply because they are Christians. That would be to introduce the notion of duty, and duty in the context of reconciliation is a denial of the kind of love which God has for human beings. Christ did not embrace the human condition out of a sense of duty. He did so out of love, the kind of love which invites the same uncomplicated and unconditional generosity in response. This is the kind of love which two people who have quarrelled feel in the split second of realizing that the quarrel has to end because they love each other – a kind of 'let's not do this any more' thought which flashes between them and which allows reconciliation to begin. God's love is an eternity of 'let's not do this any more' when it comes to the way his relationship with human beings is marred by conflict. Christians are invited to hold on to this moment of wanting to be reconciled, both with God and with one another, and to build on it. So I have written this book as a way of exploring how we might get ourselves into a place, in our minds and hearts, where this would be possible.

Each of the eight chapters looks at ways in which Christians can experience God in Jesus Christ by rediscovering him in their relationships with other Christians. In writing this book, I have found myself walking down paths which I hope others will discover, paths towards a more contemplative experience of what it really means to be a Christian community, to be the Church. But this is not a book which gives instructions. Instead, I hope that it will help readers know that it is God himself doing the work of peace-making. So it is a book for people who want a different kind of Church, a Church which takes risks and is prepared to move forward into a deeper relationship with Christ, a Church whose members are prepared to learn each other's faith language so that Christians can begin to have real conversations, the kind which foster understanding and through which everyone learns instead of one or other party simply winning the argument.

Much of the discussion turns on the notion of hospitality, God's hospitality to us in Christ reflected in the way we learn to pray and work together. Being open to the hospitality of God teaches us to be hospitable to one another, to be willing to go out to meet the other Christian long before he or she arrives on our doorstep. This involves going to the very limits, to the very edge of our individual faith universe. It takes us to the peripheries of human life in relation to God, to where holiness is learned.[1] Holiness comes with taking risks for the sake of love, so it embodies the will for reconciliation. Those who are considering coming to church for the first time, or who may be returning to their faith after a prolonged absence, will be looking for signs of this kind of holiness because they will be looking for reconciliation with God. They will be attracted to people who remind them of God's love for them, not because of the things these Christians say, but because they are a certain kind of people, a reconciled people, who remind others of Christ.

The book is also written for people who are journeying on in the Christian faith. Anyone who is asking questions, and wanting to look at issues which have the potential for bringing us closer together in new ways, is journeying on in faith. I myself have journeyed from being a Roman Catholic to becoming an Anglican. The hospitality of Anglicanism rescued me from the bleak agnosticism of early adulthood and remains the bedrock on which I continue to build and rebuild my own relationship with God and with other Christians. People who are journeying across denominational borders, or between different churchmanships, are not journeying away from their faith but looking for new ways of understanding it, ways which will give meaning and substance to their relationships with other Christians and to their lives now. They show the Church that movement in the Spirit and experience of God are still possible, so they are torch-bearers for reconciliation.

Christians inspire confidence when they are unselfconsciously like Christ in being fully themselves in their relationships, both with God and with others. This book explores how we can reconnect as a Christian community with one another with integrity and truthfulness and so become the kind of people we are meant to be, the people Christ sees from the vantage point of the cross. It is a book for those who want to experience the kind of peace which is found through friendship with the God we see in Jesus, and with other Christians, and who want to see the Church become what it really is, the ultimate place of reconciliation and belonging.

1

Can't see – won't see

————•◦•————

I knew a dog once, called Tonto. Tonto was a hefty Alsatian who lived in a rather cramped flat in Madrid. He had only one way of dealing with people or situations which he didn't like, which was to position himself so that he couldn't see them, either by facing the wall or by standing under the nearest table. The fact that he was fully visible seemed not to bother him. He would just stand there with his back turned pretending that the situation did not exist and that whoever was shouting at him would give up and go away. Tonto's logic worked on the principle that if he wasn't making eye contact, he couldn't be seen.

There is something Tonto-like in the way Christians are going about their life together. We seem to have developed a way of telling ourselves that we can't see the Christians who we don't understand. But we know they are there and they make us anxious. Being in a room with someone who makes us anxious means we find it hard to start a conversation because anxiety makes it difficult to understand or relate to what is said. In the case of the Christian community this inability to connect with other Christians has one very serious consequence. It makes us wonder if we are all worshipping the same God. How you relate to God will depend on the direction you're coming from, and there are all sorts of ways of approaching him, usually with their own built-in customs, which are foreign to some, or terms and conditions, which are reprehensible to others. But other Christians are there. It is no use pretending they will go away if ignored. So it would be good if we could understand them better and grow together, rather than apart.

The 'other' Christians are those who think differently about God and what it means to be a Christian at all. For those who resent the inevitable restrictions which come with trying not to offend other people, the difficulty in engaging with these others lies in pretending that their own questions about God and his real meaning and purpose for their lives today are irrelevant, so shouldn't be asked. Stifling doubts and questions makes the room feel even more cramped, so the solution is to find a different room where, hopefully, greater allowance is made for honest questions about God, and where there is more space in which to grow spiritually. After a while, this room also begins to feel cramped because although initially its general layout offers a certain freedom, or at least a change from the overfamiliar, the people in it are facing the wall – a different wall, but a wall all the same.

In their different groupings, Christians are hiding from each other. They feel mutually threatened because the way one group or churchmanship worships, and the way it thinks, questions the other's views, or their ways of approaching God in prayer. Those who feel alienated by liturgy or formal prayers, and by teaching which is not overtly scriptural, ignore or resent Christians who they fear might be 'unsound'. Others find charismatic worship which is without a sacramental focus shallow and wordy, despite its fervour and sincerity, and the teaching in these churches narrow and out of touch. The shock comes later when everyone discovers that God is at home in both these contexts. God makes himself at home with us in whatever church environment we happen to be, in the abiding Spirit of Jesus Christ, because God's nature is to be hospitable. There is a hospitable ethic at work in the three persons of the Trinity and this ought to inform the way Christians pray and how they relate to one another. For the time being, however, I want to focus on the fact that everyone, in order to grow into maturity, needs to turn

away from the wall, or come out from under the table, and let
God lead them – possibly to a different room altogether.

Moving into another room

I recently met a former Roman Catholic who had left the Catholic
Church because he felt that the Church was beginning to
obscure his view of God. He needed to move to a room where
he could see God more easily. As a university chaplain I welcomed
a number of Christians who had become disillusioned with
their church or denomination because of the politicization
of its life, either through issue-driven agendas which judged
and thereby excluded certain people, or because the energy it
needed in order to deepen its spiritual life was being diverted
into committee-driven approaches to problems raised by lack
of resources and general low self-confidence. Many of these
people no longer go to church but are becoming increasingly
attracted to a more contemplative approach to thinking about
what it means to be Christian community in the world of today.
There is a yearning right across the church spectrum for a
deeper, more contemplative life. People still want the sense of
belonging which a church or fellowship can give, but they want
greater depth, the space in which to discover a deeper meaning
to their faith so that they can address the uncertainties and
difficult choices which life presents with steadiness of heart and
with confidence in their ability to make choices which derive
from a living relationship with God.

According to figures quoted in the *Church Times*, 95 per cent
of people who are 'unchurched', those who like Jesus and his
teaching but distrust or dislike the institutional Church, would
want to be part of a community in which they could feel loved
and where they could experience a sense of belonging.[1] The
article goes on to say that the largest group of Christians in the
UK consists of those who do not formally belong to any one
denomination or attend any particular church. They are the

'de-churched', those who once were part of a formal church setting or wider church group. They too are searching for deeper meaning in their faith journeys. They want their Christian faith to connect with their lives in a way which is honest and relevant. These people, and those who are already part of lay contemplative or semi-contemplative communities, are people of integrity.[2] All of them, whether or not they are members of new Christian communities, are seeking God. Some will be picking up the faith of their childhood in a desire to make sense of it in their adult life. Others will be beginning again, or at least venturing further afield in a faith journey which has been uninterrupted for a number of years. These are courageous forward movements into a deeper life of faith, into another room in God's house (John 14.2).

Here I want to be clear about what I mean by faith. I do not mean clinging to what has been learned in the past, in whatever church context that may have occurred. The faith of one who needs to move on is essentially dynamic. It moves forward. It is not about standing still and facing the wall in a Tonto-like way, but about turning around in order to see God better. 'Turning around' in order to face God is also the root meaning of repentance in the Bible. Repentance, or change of heart, begins with looking at other Christians and oneself with a degree of compassionate detachment and then journeying on together. Christians are on a journey of compassionate repentance, so they need that detachment for two reasons. It obliges them to be kind to themselves, so that they can learn to forgive themselves as well as one another. It also prevents guilt and fear from getting in the way of beginning the journey at all.[3]

Moving on in faith means sitting light to the things of the past, but it does not mean shedding the old faith like a worn-out set of clothes, even though old ways of thinking and living the Christian life may feel ill-fitting or dated. Jesus likens a person's faith journey to a householder who is having a good clear-out of the attic. The householder does not throw out everything that is old. She keeps only what is fit for purpose. On the whole, this doesn't mean that the things thrown out were never of any use, or that things ought to be kept because they are new and have never been used, like unwanted Christmas presents. The householder is simply reviewing the changing needs of the household.

The Christian community is a household on the move. Its needs change, so it too must change if it is to thrive and serve in a changing world. Over the centuries the Church has undergone enormous theological changes. In her book *The Great Emergence*, Phyllis Tickle describes how these theological clear-outs occur roughly every five hundred years.[4] While history may not be so tidy, we should expect change and look to change ourselves, in order to keep moving on within our faith journeys. But first I want to be clear about why I think movement and change are so important to a healthy faith. People who move across boundaries in their faith journeys are acknowledging the fact that they can learn from those around them. They are moving on from the security of being surrounded by those who think in the same way, and towards others in a desire to understand and learn from them. Timothy Radcliffe writes, 'Because of the deep insecurity of our society, we seek the assurance of the like-minded. But no community of the like-minded is a sign of the kingdom of God.'[5] There is no such thing as a self-sufficient solitary Christian, so Christian community not only needs all its members, but thrives on diversity and forward movement.

We are involved with other Christians and, for that matter, with all people of faith. Unlike Tonto the dog, the journeying Christian is facing away from the wall and into the room. Two important things emerge from this; the first, that in turning away from the wall, we are acknowledging the fact that we belong in a space which we share with others, and the second, that we also know that the other people in the room want the same thing as we do, which is to know God better and to be known by him. These two priorities belong together, so everyone has to learn to appreciate the different ways we know and love the same God. The Christian's faith journey is not about opting out of one Christian community in order to join another. It is about opting in, in order to learn and witness to the faith in a way which enables greater understanding between Christians and which will in turn make Christianity more credible. Those who are reaching out to other Christians are therefore acting in a prophetic way.

Opting in to the conversation

Being prophetic begins with deciding whether or not we want to belong in a wider Christian context, whether or not we want to take part in the wider conversation about what it means to be a Christian. Conversation has rightly been described as an art. It takes time and practice to become a good conversational partner, one who listens with a real desire to learn and understand from another person. Neither the person who dominates the dinner table by hectoring or lecturing everyone else, nor the one who remains obstinately silent, is a good conversational partner. Both are blocking the productive exchange of ideas, the process in which everyone stands to gain in learning something from the conversation as a whole. Real conversation takes place between people who want to know and understand something together and, in the process, know and understand one another. It is not simply a matter of dragging someone else around to my way of thinking, or of one person shoring up his self-confidence with the sound of his own voice, while another opts out either from boredom or because she feels undervalued. Real conversation involves risk because it requires that all involved shed old and comfortable opinions and be prepared to have their minds 're-formed'. Good conversation is not about winning arguments. In fact all parties need to 'lose' the argument in order to be able to learn from it together and move on to something new.

Losing arguments is about losing one's life in order to gain it (Matt. 10.39 and parallels). When Jesus talks about this loss of life, he is saying that in order to grow and learn we need to 'lose' the outworn values and opinions which shaped and propped up the old self, but which are no longer fit for purpose because they can no longer generate new ideas or allow the discussion to be informed by love. They may sound authoritative but they also alienate. When this happens, the conversation becomes a sparring match between individuals who are defending the cherished opinions which keep them independent and separate from one another. No one really needs anyone else's contribution so there is nothing new to be learned. The silent person senses this and gives up on the situation. She faces the wall, like Tonto, so as not to have to take anything new on board or get caught in the crossfire. Her reluctance to get involved allows the conversation to degenerate into all-out war in which all that matters is being right and winning. The remaining participants sense this and the argument ratchets up a notch or two. They are now just as Tonto-like as the silent onlooker because they have lost sight of the real person behind the one who is angrily defending his position. This is where all parties need to lose the argument in order to be able to learn from it and move on.

For this to be possible, those involved need to 'see' their fellow guests, and this requires the ability to engage with them, to understand and, if possible, speak their language. It involves skill and trust. Instead of facing the wall, all those around the table now face one another. They do this by moving away from their own personal isolationism and trying to connect with different ways of apprehending God and with how these in turn inform the way others understand and voice the problem being discussed. Difference therefore matters. It becomes the basis for creativity because of the love that has been allowed to soften it and so make it more malleable, more able to be shaped into new ways of thinking and speaking about God.

Learning new languages

Timothy Radcliffe, who was a Dominican monk, tells a story of Saint Dominic, the founder of the Dominican Order, who, while on his travels, found himself preaching to a group of Germans. Dominic did not speak German and remarked to his companion that he felt frustrated at not being able to communicate with them. He prayed that he might learn to understand his German listeners, so that he and his companion might communicate the gospel more effectively. Dominic wanted to share with them from a place of common understanding. As a result, his preaching, like all good preaching, became a creative conversation, one in which he tried to understand and communicate in the faith language of his listeners.[6] Dominic was looking for a way to listen and understand others by engaging with them at a deeper level than words can take us.

C. S. Lewis, at the end of his book *The Last Battle*, speaks of the ultimate purpose of human existence as moving 'further up and further in'. He is describing the Christian's journey towards God and into God's life. It is a relational journeying, not a solo flight. We travel both further 'up' towards God and one another and further 'in', into the unknown, the unspoken, into God's life and love, as we also encounter it in one another. Going further up involves being prepared to travel and learn in our ongoing relationship with God and with other Christians. Going further in is about being consciously still in order to hear and understand God's purpose and to learn more about him through the ways in which other Christians speak of him.

Many people who are moving across churchmanships are looking for ways to extend their theological horizons and deepen their prayer life, but they do not necessarily want to do this in private. They sense that other Christians, who are also members of the worshipping body of Christ, have treasures to offer which they previously were only vaguely aware existed. These new searchers, many of them long-standing members of their own churches, are exploring other churchmanships in order to experience God more deeply in the way other Christian groupings think and worship. They are finding that crossing existing boundaries opens up a way into a deeper Church, one which offers them the space in which to know and be known by God and so reach a better understanding of the full picture, what it means to be a Christian alongside other Christians. When Christians meet in this space, they meet Jesus Christ, but it is also a space where differences are felt most keenly, a space for division rather than encounter. In the next chapter I shall be looking at how Christians might learn to meet in a new space in his name, and share his peace.

Questions to reflect on and discuss

- Do you have any close Christian friends who are not from your church or denomination?
- If not, why do you suppose that is?
- If you do, what is the most significant aspect of that friendship for you personally?
- What aspects of the friendship challenge you the most?

2

Jesus? Or Christ?
On becoming bilingual

Jesus was a focus for conflict and controversy. He said that he had come 'not to bring peace, but a sword' (Matt. 10.34). The religious authorities accused him of being subversive because they felt threatened by his words and his presence. He touched people at their centre, the deepest or truest part of the human spirit. In questioning outworn values and priorities he offered them freedom by inviting them into a new way of living in relationship, both with God and with one another.

Emerging Church – living out the freedom

Today's Christians are invited to live out this freedom, but like those early disciples they also must question old values and assumptions as they seek Jesus Christ in modern life and in the issues and controversies which divide us. The problem for Christians is that the conversation has stalled because we don't know how to engage with difference. In fact Christians are, on the whole, rather afraid of difference, so they only hold conversations with the like-minded, with those who speak their particular faith language and with whom they feel comfortable because they agree about the grammar which makes that language intelligible.

As a university chaplain who was trying to get both Protestant and Catholic Christians to engage with one another and eventually work together, I was constantly aware of a fundamental, yet seldom mentioned, area of difference: that one group worshipped Jesus and the other Christ in a way which made each name feel like a loyalty badge. It led to an implicit labelling of people. There were the 'evangelicals' who did everything for Jesus and were enormously proactive in getting the chaplaincy known on campus, and there were the 'Anglicans' who had Eucharists and Compline and who talked about Christ. These Christ-centred Christians made the chaplaincy into a safe space in which those who were journeying between denominations or churches could ask questions about the faith and challenge outworn assumptions. My concern was that the chaplaincy should allow both names, and that their use should become a positive unifying factor. For this to happen, people were going to have to relearn the art of conversation. They were going to have to risk getting out of their identity comfort zones by learning to listen to and understand each other's faith language.

Learning new languages – are Christians meant to be more than friends?

If how we think about Jesus Christ, and how we identify with his name, is to be a unifying factor, we have to understand what that name signifies to each member of a Christian community, so that all parties to the conversation can learn. It is about developing ways of talking about God and of being a Christian community which enable Christians to relate to one another in a more meaningful way. It involves developing a particular kind of friendship which connects us with one another at a deeper level, the level at which we encounter Jesus Christ together. So faith language is not simply about agreeing on certain non-negotiable articles of faith or moral issues, significant as these may be, but about making connections with other Christians, as well as with people who seek to know God through other faith journeys. In this chapter I want to explore this idea a little further and later, in the next chapter, describe some contexts in which learning to speak and understand another's faith language prepares us for the work of reconciliation.

Many of us know what it is like to go on holiday abroad without ever having learned the language. The frustration is not just a matter of not understanding the menu and not being confident that we have ordered the food we think we're ordering. It has to do with failing to connect with another person, whether it is the one who brings the food, or others at the table. To speak another language fluently is to understand what makes a person 'tick', so it is about engaging with the potential for the kind of understanding which underpins friendship and ultimately leads to trust. Those who speak another language fluently, especially if they have learned it in early childhood, can get into the mindset and imagination of others and begin to see things the way they do. Bilingual people can see and experience the world in the way these others do by identifying with their particular culture-conditioned experience. They can think of the other person as a 'thou'.

In Mediterranean languages, addressing someone as 'thou', or *tu*, implies informality and friendship. In his book *I and Thou* Martin Buber writes, 'Every great culture that comprehends nations rests on an original relational incident, on a response to the *Thou* made at its source.'[1] When a Christian learns to speak the faith language of someone coming from another churchmanship, he or she begins to relate to the other Christian as a 'thou'. Together, they establish a real connection and can begin to communicate from that deeper level of understanding which is the 'source' of their relationship.

Making connections

Understanding and interpreting the world in the language of others leads to a level of understanding which goes beyond translation because it allows us to sense the meaning of things in a different way without the need for translation or complicated explanations. We begin to understand others by discovering that we hold something in common. We enjoy their food not only because it tastes delicious, but because they enjoy it too. Our shared enjoyment tells us something about them as people and invites us into their world and into their way of enjoying it. It is this shared enjoyment, rather than just the food itself, which makes for good memories, and good memories make for enduring connections.

Memories of extended holiday lunches in congenial company rekindle our connectedness with the people and country visited. These memories may also be associated with certain words or expressions, so the language enriches the memory, rather than being simply a barrier. It brings it back to life. It is regenerative. The history of God's dealings with his people is like these memories. His word is a language which regenerates: he has promised that it will not return to him empty (Isa. 55.11). When Christians move outside familiar church surroundings and begin to engage with others because they want to understand them, and to enrich their own faith in doing so, they are part of this ongoing regenerative process.

As Christians, we need to learn to understand God's language in new ways and in the ways other Christians understand it, allowing our experience of him to be enriched by theirs, so that his voice and the meaning of his word in Scripture do not return to him empty. Those who have to preach sermons know how important it is to have people who can read the lessons set for that Sunday intelligently and sensitively. Too often we hear someone we know well adopting a 'churchy' voice when called upon to read aloud from the Bible. This does not help the preacher and probably conveys very little of the deeper meaning of the text to the congregation, so God's word returns to him empty. Reading which communicates meaning comes after prayerful preparation. In the next chapter I shall be looking at how we can engage with texts more deeply and so discover for ourselves a deeper and richer meaning of Scripture.

In order to understand one another better, Christians try to be real when they join with others in reading Scripture or in worship. By this I mean being oneself first and evangelical or Anglican later, if at all. Learning to understand others in the way they speak about God also means listening more deeply to what is being read, so we try to make this easier for one another by not adopting either a 'churchy' Anglican voice or an 'upbeat' evangelical voice. We try to listen and pray together as the people we are. We begin to do this by listening to the language of others, how they fashion words into ways of worshipping and speaking about God which resonate with their understanding of him, but which are also true to who they are as people we know in daily life, outside the church context. As we listen in this way, we begin to understand subtleties and have a better sense of the meaning of what they are saying. It is like understanding someone from another country, or being bilingual.

Getting dual nationality

None of this is easy. On the whole, the English find it hard to learn a new language, partly because we assume that everyone speaks English. The English in particular, as opposed to the Welsh, Scottish and Irish, expect others to learn English. In contrast to the practice in Wales, the Netherlands and Scandinavia, the English do not attempt to meet others halfway by teaching a foreign language at nursery school, or playgroup, before a child enters the formal education system.

The English are also easily embarrassed. We don't like to make fools of ourselves in front of people we don't know very well, so the only way to overcome embarrassment, where languages are concerned, lies in a desire to be friends with those we are trying to engage with, rather than just dismissing them as 'foreign'. It is not just a matter of making oneself understood by speaking more slowly, or by shouting, like the hotel proprietor in *Fawlty*

Towers, but about wanting to communicate at 'source', where the real person is. It is about becoming bilingual to the point where we can have more than one nationality and still remain the same person.

As Christians, we are often embarrassed and impatient when we have to worship or speak about the Christian faith in the company of those whose faith language is quite different from our own, or whose worship we find tedious or trite, so we try to block out what we would rather not hear or engage with. We put on sound-protection headphones. While this may make it possible for everyone to remain in the same room, it also blocks understanding because it does not allow the real meaning of what is being said to penetrate to our own 'source', the place where we meet the Christ who says 'thou' to us. Muffling other Christians' faith language reduces it to an annoying background noise, like the noise on the other side of the wall which divides one flat from another. We remain in our own room and they in theirs.

Christians are like people living in a block of flats with very thin walls. Noise from upstairs or next door can be annoying but can also be the means of establishing better relations. I once lived in New York, in an apartment block where my upstairs neighbour played rather good music, which was only partly audible but loud enough to be annoying if you lived below him. So we considered the idea of piping his excellent recordings of a band he was currently working with (he was a sound engineer) down the air-conditioning duct, so that we could both enjoy it to maximum effect and at mutually agreed times. We never actually did this but we did become friends. So thin walls and poor sound insulation can have their uses. Perhaps there is a way in which we could think about the walls which separate Christians as walls supporting the same building. The walls may be rather thin in places but they may also have built-in useful elements for sharing and celebrating something or someone we love – provided, of course, we are celebrating and loving the same person and the same God.

Loving the same God

Paul likens the Christian Church to a building (1 Cor. 3.9). It is God's building, so good conversation between Christians is about building something together, not for ourselves, but for God. As fellow builders, we are obliged to forget about individual interests and separate church agendas in order to connect with one another, so that we can understand God together and learn his purpose. God's purpose is that the building should function properly and not collapse. As good builders, we must learn one another's faith language so that we can communicate, because when builders don't communicate the building project fails.

There was a real estate developer in Ibiza in the early sixties, when the island was virtually unknown, who wanted to create easy access to the sea from his newly built hotel, but who made the mistake of dealing with two contractors. The contractors disagreed on how the road should be built. Each team did things their own way and they ended up, inevitably, with two roads, one leading into a cliff face and the other plunging the hapless driver down several hundred feet into the sea. If Christians are not more willing to build together by communicating and connecting in their shared love for God, we shall end up with a number of roads leading nowhere. Christians need to learn new languages in order to work more productively, so that their separate roads converge on the same destination and they meet in Jesus Christ.

We meet in his name

The problem lies not in our travelling along different roads, but in our destination: we fail to meet as a single people in the name we share. The failure is caused by the way we understand the name Jesus Christ, and this can lead us to inflict pain on one another. Once again, this can be traced to how we read Scripture but this time it is a question of emphasis. So Scripture is either personal and inerrant, the directly inspired word of God leading to God's ultimate work of payment for human sin in the person of Jesus, or it is God's invitation to be in a renewed relationship with him through Christ.[2] For some, Jesus is the personal saviour, Emmanuel, which means 'God with us' and the Church is a community whose members have made a personal commitment to him as fully responsible adults. For others, who are equally committed but view salvation differently, Christ is the one through whom, in the words of John's Gospel, 'all things came into being' (John 1.3), the *pantocrator*, or sustainer of the universe, and the eternal *logos*, the dynamic movement of God acting in the world and on the human condition from the very beginning.[3] These Christians understand themselves to be part of the 'communion of saints', in fellowship with Christians going back through history to the very beginning of the Church's life.

The name Jesus Christ contains all these meanings. He holds these words and ideas together, and in them holds together divided Christianity. So the problem for Christians has to do with an inability to move forward in the healing process so as to become one in Jesus Christ. The situation resembles the one I described earlier in which people living in the same apartment block can choose whether or not to make the experience mutually beneficial. Different Christian churchmanships and interest groups are living in different rooms in a building supported by Jesus Christ whose name both divides and holds them together. At the same time he destroys what Paul calls 'the dividing wall, that is, the hostility between us' (Eph. 2.14). So he becomes the cornerstone which holds the walls of the building together without the need for any dividing wall. He braces the two walls against each other and holds them in place, so neither one can stand alone. Each wall needs the other and both need the cornerstone, or the building will collapse.

Whose God? Yours or mine?

The name Jesus Christ embodies what Christians are supposed to be about. He is the cornerstone which gives shape and structure to the way the Christian community understands itself and which holds it together. The two names unite different aspects of the same person, so together they ought to unite different Christians, but too often they push them apart. It is not that the names Jesus and Christ mean something different to different Christians but that some will identify with one name more than with the other and pull away from those whose faith and sense of self is shaped and held in a way that they feel concentrates on only one aspect of the Son of God. This creates a fundamental imbalance in relations between Christians, even though it is seldom recognized.

Some Christians will relate more closely to *Jesus* in his humanity while others will want to deepen into the mystery of the Godhead through contemplative prayer and the sacraments, and so find greater significance and meaning in the person of *Christ*. It is easy to dismiss these choices as a matter of mood or inclination, but something much more significant is really going on. Broadly speaking, these different ways of thinking about what it means to be Christian converge on the idea of salvation itself and on how God's grace works to effect it. In the interplay between grace and salvation, grace is a gift which energizes the life of Christian community. It energizes Christians to move forward in their faith and at the same time towards one another, rather than remaining, like Tonto the dog, under their separate tables.

Some Christians have begun this forward movement by crossing churchmanship boundaries, by exploring more contemplative ways of relating to other Christians, or by deepening their understanding of Scripture by joining different kinds of study groups. They are seeking to learn from others, so that all can begin to rediscover God, and the salvation he offers in Jesus Christ, in new and surprising ways. The Church which is emerging from the divisions of the past is doing so because people want to find Jesus Christ in ways which are alive and new. They also want reconciliation. They want to learn from one another, to know Jesus Christ as he is known by Christians of other denominations or churchmanships. They want to see the Church's mission being renewed by his Spirit from within its own life.

Questions to reflect on and discuss

- Do you describe yourself as Christian, or as Anglican, Catholic or any other denomination? What do you think is the difference?
- Have you ever had difficult neighbours? How did you deal with the situation? What did you learn from it? How might you apply the insights you gained to your relationships with other Christians? How might they be applied to the life of your church?
- What do we mean when we say we are the body of Christ?

3

'But I say to you . . .'
Re-missioning the Church

There is more to the life of Christian community than niceness and camaraderie. We are not a holy club but a vital human family called to model the love of God for the world in the way we relate to one another. God's love for us is vital and the Christian family needs this vitality to re-energize its life together. The vitality of God's love supplies the kind of energy which enables Christians to turn conflict into something new and creative, something which energizes the community from within and which enables it to learn from conflict, find healing in forgiveness and move forward.

Jesus was not known for politeness. He was certainly outspoken when it came to confronting hypocrisy and standing by the marginalized. In fact there were times when he embarrassed his friends and supporters and upset his relatives by his apparent lack of concern for their feelings. The 12-year-old in the Temple telling his distraught parents, who had been searching for him for three days, that they should have known to look for him in his Father's house was hardly the meek and mild Jesus of Victorian hymnody. Neither was the man who made a whip out of cords and drove the loan sharks out of the Temple. There was an impatience and energy about him which the religious and secular authorities found disquieting. If the Church is to rediscover this energy in the face of the world's hardness of heart, its exploitation of the weak and marginalized, it first needs to rediscover the energy of God's love, his Holy Spirit, within its own life.

Jesus said that his disciples would be recognized not just by their words and actions, but by being a certain kind of people. In both public and private life they would reveal God's love in the sincerity of their love for one another, as well as in the things they said and did. They would be known by their fruits. The problem for those who are considering becoming Christians lies in not always being able to tell which are the good fruits and which, though they may appear good from the outside, are not so good on the inside. Nothing is more disappointing than a luscious looking pear which turns out to be dry and tasteless, or than going to a new church and finding that it is just as dry and tasteless as the one you left behind. So perhaps it is time Christians of all churchmanships came together in order to find out how good we really are on the inside, whether as Christian community we are in danger of losing our flavour because we no longer convey the vital love for one another which the world so badly needs to see. Many people who are thinking of returning to church, and many of those already in it, sense that despite what we do in the way of outreach and mission, we are not moving forward ourselves. They sense a certain tiredness which at times makes us sound insincere. Something inside us is missing; we lack the energy and passionate love for people which made Jesus such an attractive person and drew others to him.

Thousands would follow Jesus in order to hear him speak or just to catch a glimpse of him. He responded to passion in others too, especially those who least expected him to do so, like Zacchaeus, the little man perched halfway up a tree who collaborated with the Roman occupying forces and made money out of his own countrymen. Jesus publicly honours him as a friend by inviting himself for supper that evening and Zacchaeus' life is transformed in a single moment (Luke 19.1–10). Jesus does the same for the woman who wipes his feet with her tears and embarrasses other guests at an elegant dinner (Luke 7.36–50). The way Jesus treated marginalized people like

Zacchaeus and this woman was his way of honouring them as friends, as people who belonged *with* him as well as to him. His treatment of them restored their belief in God because it restored their belief in themselves and in the possibility of their goodness in his sight. Jesus showed them that they mattered, that they were valuable and that their lives had a purpose.

Christians are called to treat one another in the way Jesus treated people, beginning with the Christians they find embarrassing, or who do not conform to their expectations of what a Christian should be like. Only in this way will they convince others of what Jesus means to them. They need to have a particular passion for marginalized Christians, whose humanity is often implicitly devalued. Perhaps it is time Christians started to love the weakest among them with the vitality of the love shown by a French soldier who, passing through a village in central France shortly after the Second World War, came across a group of villagers tarring and feathering a woman. The woman had been having an affair with a German officer, probably in order to protect and feed her own children. The ex-soldier was enraged at the way the villagers were dehumanizing this woman, who was a human being like them, so he intervened to stop her persecutors and restore her honour. In taking on her attackers, he reclothed her in her humanity. Christians are similarly called to be careful to protect, and where necessary restore, the honour of other Christians, their value in the eyes of God.

Honouring each other's faith

Christians don't always honour other Christians by taking care to reclothe them in their full humanity when they are mocked or criticized. This also applies in the context of disputes and arguments. The losers are just 'losers', people who are not part of the important bigger picture which others have of the Church.

If we look closely at Rembrandt's painting of the prodigal son, we see that it tells us something about how a person honours another and reclothes him by giving him back his sense of belonging, and hence his self-worth. The painting says something too about how honour is also connected to valuing the way others live out their faith and it tells us something about faith itself. The older son in his respectable but everyday clothes resents the fact that his father seems not to recognize his loyalty and devotion, and takes his dogged faithfulness for granted. As far as he is concerned, his younger brother's faith was not up to staying at home and getting on with the job of running the estate.

What the older brother perhaps does not realize is that the younger brother's faith had been worn down by the disillusionments of life. He finally lost it altogether when his friends used him for his money and dropped him when the money ran out. So he comes home naked, without any of the old faith, which failed him when he really needed it, but with a great desire for God. The father in Rembrandt's picture clothes him with the best cape and gives him the family signet ring. He reclothes the young man as an honoured son without even waiting for him to wash, as the painting so graphically portrays. The old rags he is still wearing are the old 'self'-sufficiency, the only faith he ever really had. But even that old self-faith is acknowledged by the father, who reclothes it with the new cape. He accepts and honours the young man as he is, and in what he has been, not as someone he might become in the future. The new clothes he gives to the younger son represent both a transformation of his old faith into something new and precious, and the fulfilment of what he realizes he most needs, which is to be a son again.[1]

Those who are moving into new churchmanships, or who are beginning to forge friendships with Christians who are quite different from themselves, are giving back to the Church something which many Christians have lost sight of, the regeneration of desire for God. Their own desire to experience God, to 'taste and see that the LORD is good' (Ps. 34.8), is making them look for other contexts in which they might find him, once again, and as if for the first time. It is a kind of homecoming in reverse. They are finding God in new ways, in the 'homes' of other Christians. But the will for change and for a deeper encounter with God also comes with a desire for enduring friendship with the Christians they left behind. The two belong together. Moving across churchmanship boundaries is not just about preferring one church to another. It is about journeying more deeply into God so that we can honour and be honoured by other Christians for who we are in whatever church context we find ourselves.

Blessing other Christians

When Jesus speaks of blessing and not cursing those who malign us (Luke 6.27–31), he is talking about honouring. Honouring requires sincerity if it is to be more than flattery. So by speaking of honouring others as a way of blessing them, I am not suggesting that we just say all the right things, or try to persuade ourselves that we like someone when we don't, but that we ask for the grace to see the human being in that person and to want him or her to be blessed by God. At the same time, we cannot bless those who persecute us unless we really want to see them blessed, and in order to do this, we need to see them as God sees them. This is where the work of forgiveness in the Church begins.

Forgiveness and blessing are about vulnerability. We forgive other Christians because we see ourselves in them. They are just like us. They are prone to anxiety, make the wrong kinds of friends or choose the wrong partners, and suffer the consequences, just as we all do. Forgiving and blessing other Christians is about being vulnerable to Jesus Christ alongside them in their vulnerability. It involves seeing through to the human being behind whatever label we have decided on – the 'happy clappy', the 'traditionalist', the 'liberal', or the person who is just gay, or a woman. In seeing through these labels, which hide the real person, we see the brother or sister in Christ and want to be reconciled with them.

This was the original vision of the ecumenical community at Taizé, which was founded in 1940 by Brother Roger Schütz, himself a Swiss Protestant. He had spent much of the war in Switzerland, and wanted to see neutrality become a positive force for reconciliation. A former student at Cardiff University told us of a moment of reconciliation which she witnessed at Taizé. She gave it as an example of how Taizé breaks down barriers. 'There were,' she said, 'many such moments – usually Catholic/Protestants getting to know one another, openly discussing what makes us different and yet the same, and becoming friends, realizing that these differences are tiny when it comes to our true faith.'

The student described this moment in the following way: 'The most interesting thing that happened to me was meeting an American couple from a Catholic/Baptist background who had started going to an independent charismatic church. They stood out the most from us others who were mostly Catholic, Lutheran, or Baptist, because they weren't on speaking terms with their family and friends at home. They had stopped speaking to them because they no longer agreed with Catholics or Baptists – or any formal church. One day we got into a heated argument. I said they wouldn't be in Taizé and taking part in this programme if they disrespected everyone else. As the conversation calmed down, the couple realized that they had personal issues with the people they weren't talking to which had nothing to do with the Church . . . Taizé is a learning experience for both sides, those who don't know people from different denominations, and those who do, but choose to leave a certain church because of some bad experiences and generalizations. These are often about churches vying for more followers. In the end we were like one big family (which is what I love most about Taizé), and celebrated the Easter liturgy together.'

Brother Roger died in 2005, but his original vision lives on because people go to Taizé and find reconciliation and forgiveness with other Christians, often without expecting or feeling the need for either when they first arrive. They discover it while they are there and in doing so, as the story shows, they begin to experience what it is like to be God's forgiven people, the brothers and sisters of other Christians who are also forgiven. The story shows how reconciliation and forgiveness within the Christian community takes place in the context of conversation, even if the conversation turns into an argument. Listening to others when we disagree with them is a way of blessing them. Sometimes we have to stay with the argument – something which is especially difficult for those who tend to shy off confrontation – and endure conflict in order to arrive together at a different place, one in which we see others as if we were meeting them for the first time, and in so doing experience God himself in a new way.

'Bless and do not curse' – living and worshipping as a forgiven people

Anyone who has visited Taizé will know that worshipping God with large numbers of Christians of different nationalities and denominations is challenging in many ways, but in it we experience God. At Taizé we call on God together and he meets us as his people, not as separate groups, as charismatic evangelicals or Anglo-Catholics. Many of the services take place in a tent, open on all four sides in the summer. In this huge space, alongside a thousand or more young Christians, we experience God very closely.

The Taizé community orchestrates the worship in such a way as to make sure of this sense of God's presence. Having so many people in what now feels like quite an intimate space means that only a few will get a good view of what is going on, but after one or two songs the entire congregation turns around so that the people who thought they were at the back now have an altar, or a worship leader, right in front of them. There are a number of these altars, or focus points, so by the end of the service everyone has at some point experienced being at the front.

This is a powerful illustration of what it means to be Christian community in the context of worship. First, because the very act of turning around resonates with the idea of *metanoia*, the turning around of the self in repentance. At Taizé people experience a collective *metanoia*, in which everyone takes responsibility for the whole Christian community's estrangement from God and, through shared worship and informal conversation, confronts its divisions and jealously guarded identities. Second, because in turning around and in singing in different national languages, those present experience what it is to speak the same language, the language of love and praise, to the same God. The language of praise breaks boundaries and unites people, and so blesses them, as well as honouring God himself. This blessing of praise takes them into uncharted waters beyond the familiar and cosy to a new and entirely different place, one which is new to everyone because it is being experienced for the first time. So in our worship we learn a new language together, one which everyone can speak.

Taizé is a reminder of how God reaches out with unconditional love to meet those who seek him, as they try to understand and love other Christians by learning their faith language, something which may also entail having to learn a little of their ordinary human language as well. At Taizé a lot of time is spent just sitting around and talking. Friendships develop because people discover they like each other. There is a mutual attraction, like that between Christ and the people he met as he journeyed up and down the Holy Land. Students who have visited Taizé have said that friendships often begin in the most ordinary moments, like laughing at the same funny story, finding that you are studying the same subject at university, or discovering common likes and dislikes.

While these conversations prepare the ground for friendship, people also come up against difference, as in the case of the couple just mentioned. What is significant about that story is not only the fact that the argument was finally resolved, but that everyone learned something about themselves and about each other. There were no winners or losers. Instead, they realized that the issue of churchmanship was part of a much larger and more complex one, which had to do with the history of the individuals concerned and their relationships with other people. The negative feelings generated by these dysfunctional relationships fed into how the two people felt about their churches. The result was a reactive movement away from their families, rather than a proactive movement towards them, and a defensive attitude towards the other students at Taizé. They distrusted the other students on the basis of denomination or churchmanship, rather than for the people they were. During the course of the conversation with the Cardiff student and her friends, the couple were able to see the truth of the situation and start to relearn trust by engaging with them as fellow human beings and fellow Christians.

The conversation which the Cardiff student had at Taizé is a good example of how it is possible for Christians to listen to and honour the faith journeys of other Christians by getting alongside them without bias or judgement and loving them where they are. To get alongside other people in this way is to bless them. We bless those we disagree with or dislike by being vulnerable to God's love ourselves and trusting that it will reach them through us, without our having to do anything at all except see them in their humanity and want their greatest happiness, their greatest good. This is a very important consideration when thinking about the sort of contentious issues which divide Christians today, issues which relate to how we read Scripture and interpret the truth.

Questions to reflect on and discuss

- Is your church or fellowship losing its original flavour? Is it becoming dry and tasteless on the inside? What do you think it lacks? How might you go about changing the situation?
- Are there divisions in your church or fellowship? How might you go about blessing those you don't understand or with whom you disagree? Think back to the last disagreement you had with them. What do you wish you had said or done? What would you like them to do for you?
- How do you feel when someone has the last word in an argument over how Scripture is interpreted in relation to a particular issue? How do you think about such people when you pray for them? Do you just wish they would change?

4

Whose truth is it anyway?

————•◦•————

When an artist paints a picture does she know why she is painting it? Paintings, and indeed photographs, are more than pictures of something. Paintings grow over time. They take shape through a kind of dialogue which goes on between the artist and the painting and which will be picked up and developed by the viewer long after the artist has finished working on it. The dialogue becomes an invitation to the viewer to enter into a situation and become part of it, so the painting is a living organic work, inviting further questions and speculation as to the precise circumstances and reasons for its existence.

Think, for example, of the painting *Las Meninas* by Velásquez. The young princess, the Infanta Margharita, and her attendants look at the viewer as if they are pausing for a moment to ask, 'What are you doing here?' The painter is also looking at the viewer, as if he had been interrupted in his work, possibly by the arrival of the Infanta's parents who we see reflected in a mirror at the back of the room and who may or may not be the subject of another painting. So we have at least two moments captured within a single picture. Velásquez creates a space in which the viewer can return the gaze of the Infanta and her companions, and in so doing allows the viewer to capture and contemplate a single and precise moment in the life of a royal household in seventeenth-century Spain, thereby transforming it, in all its complexity, into a single shared reality.

The artist has captured a truth in this moment which will be shared across the span of generations, connecting artist, viewers and subjects to one another within a single reality, but he has not defined the truth in precise terms. The truth, or moment, will resonate differently with different viewers, just as it will have been experienced in different ways by the subjects in the picture.

Truth and the art of conversation

This brief description of Velásquez's painting is only an indication of how artists pursue truth and of what also draws people to paintings. We want to connect and make sense of intuitions relating to the human predicament, intuitions which we perhaps never knew we had. It is also why writers tell stories and write books.[1] Artists invite us to join with them in a search for shared meaning through the language of colour, shape and form and, in doing so, to make sense of truth. Paintings use memory and association to help us arrive at certain truths about ourselves and the world around us, truths which may develop over time as the viewer gets to know the picture better, or which will strike one person in a particular way but may not be recognizable to another viewing the same picture. Both viewers will have to make sense of the picture through how they receive the impressions which it creates. So although it may initially appear to be the same picture to everyone who sees it, it may also convey different meanings to different viewers, meanings which even the artist may not have thought of.

The way I have chosen to describe the Velásquez painting is only one way of viewing it, but it suggests that paintings allow truth to deepen and develop through a kind of implicit conversation between the artist and the viewer which is mediated by the painting itself. Artists paint (and here I speak as someone who spent a number of years painting pictures) because there is something in *the moment of seeing* which compels us to try to grasp the significance of that moment in a way that words alone cannot. If we apply this method for connecting with truth to how Christians receive and then convey the truth to others, it reveals one very significant lack. Christians do not always have a light touch when it comes to describing their beliefs. They are a little afraid of using their imagination in order to reinterpret Christian truth for the world and the Church of today in a meaningful way, so they often say too much. They leave little space for the silence of not knowing.[2]

One of the great strengths which Jesus has as a teacher is the way he is able to use stories and allegories, or verbal paintings, to connect with people. Imagination reveals truth because it connects with people where they are and often allows for a degree of ambiguity, of not quite knowing what is being said. The stories Jesus tells often ask questions, or elicit questions from his listeners, questions which make them think again and so rediscover a truth they had perhaps always known but never really faced. While the parables and stories which Jesus tells are often used to make a single point for a given time, they also allow for future retelling. People will be able to read the stories again and again, in different social contexts and in different times in history, and discover their truth in new ways.

Jesus also shapes his stories and parables so that those who read them in an unbiased and non-defensive way can recognize themselves in the characters, or identify with the situations. In this sense, the parables are a conversation about truth. They are visual moments which are more than illustrations of a point. They draw us in and, in so doing, oblige us to re-engage with the truth of the story and, if necessary, allow our perception of that truth to change and develop. They implicate us in the outcome of the parable 'conversation', which is why they so often draw on real life situations. They reveal a truth about who we are and are inherently dramatic, designed for a purpose, like the staging of a piece of theatre.

The staging and design of plays and musicals reveal truth, often by involving the audience directly with what is happening on stage. Harold Prince's definitive 1968 production of *Cabaret*, designed by Boris Aronson, confronts the audience with a mirror running the full width of the stage. Those watching see themselves reflected in the mirror at various points during the performance. They become part of the truth being played out on stage. In seeing itself as part of the action and of the set itself, the audience is drawn into the decadence and nihilism which shaped German society in the 1920s and which helped to generate Nazism. The set reinforces the truth which the play is dealing with – that willingly or not, we are all implicated in what is done in our name by those who hold political or economic power, even though we may be unaware of this at the time.

Living truth

The examples I have given, drawing on classical painting and modern theatre, suggest that Christians often miss a trick when it comes to dealing with truth. We fail to respect the truth for what it is: an organic reality bound up with who we are, difficult to define but for which we can and should take some creative responsibility. Christians are called to 'witness' to the truth of God by engaging with truth as it is worked out in the web of complex questions and situations which have brought us to where we are today. So perhaps we ought to think about truth in the way the artist thinks of it while working on a painting. The artist allows truth to emerge during the working process. She does not force it to become something other than it is, or wants to be. The artist knows that if the truth is to emerge, or be revealed, as she works, she must not get in its way by imposing her personality or particular truth agenda onto the painting. Instead, she must allow it to 'speak' to her. When she does this, her real character, the truth about her rather than her personality, will be revealed within the truth she is describing.

If we think of Scripture as a kind of ongoing painting, we see that its truth also bears the mark of the different characters who wrote it, and of our own in the way we read it and pass on its truth to others. We have a creative involvement with, and responsibility to, that truth. But this does not give us permission to manipulate Scripture in order to enhance one idea or downplay another so as to contain it within safe and secure boundaries. We do not have permission to force God's word to be something other than it is, a living and dynamic truth pointing to God's salvation, which is 'working', as Jesus himself says, up to and including the present moment (John 5.17).

Allowing Scripture its own life allows us to discern and make sense of truth in the difficult realities of human experience. The whole thrust of Scripture points to a central truth, which is that God chooses to be involved in that experience. He chooses to heal and forgive from within his own life. So when Christians speak of truth, they are speaking of the acceptance and forgiveness offered to them in the self-giving of Jesus, who is the heartbeat of God's life, the truth of God made real.

Learning each other's truth language

This means that the truth of God and the love of God belong together. It follows that if Christians are going to talk about truth, they need to begin by thinking of it as something which holds them together within that love, rather than allowing it to push them apart. They need to think of it as that which is revealed in the kind of commonality discovered by the students at Taizé, and in conversations in which everybody has taken the trouble to learn and understand each other's truth language. Through learning each other's truth language, as I suggested in the second chapter of this book, Christians begin to understand the subtleties and nuances of each other's *experiences* of truth. Since the Church consists of a living body of people who speak different truth languages, it needs to rediscover truth as something living and organic. A living organic truth is one which helps us make sense of our changing lives and of ourselves as a diverse people who are held together within God's greater truth, within his love, a love which leads to deeper understanding. Problems arise because on the whole we do not dare give truth the freedom it needs for this deeper understanding to become possible.

Managing truth

The problem begins when we try to apply these ideas to our life together in the midst of the spiritual and moral challenges of a rapidly changing and complex world. At this point, truth has to be free to grow in the context of history, science and technology and all the other kinds of knowledge and experience which human beings have acquired. It also has to remain faithful to the gospel, which reveals the truth as embodied in the life, death and resurrection of Jesus Christ. What is most challenging about this is not that we need to arrive at a set of definitive answers to what is or is not true in order to justify our Christian faith, but that we have to love unconditionally. In other words, we have to find a way of loving other Christians and the world itself which takes us beyond the 'true' or 'false' and which is capable of riding the waves of subjective feelings about groups or individuals. We have to love truthfully.

This understanding of truth is difficult for most of us because it appears to lead to the conclusion, on the one hand, that when it comes to faith 'anything goes' as long as we love each other and, on the other, that nothing can really be said to be true because we know little about what Jesus actually said and taught since we only have a selection of his teachings to draw on, some of which seem to be at odds with other parts of Scripture. But it is probably fair to say that the majority of Christians have a sense of the deep truth of the gospel. The problem lies in the difficulties we encounter when it comes to sharing that deep truth in different ways. Many Christians respond to the truth dilemma by either selecting bits of Scripture which appear to endorse a particular truth agenda in relation to a specific issue, and in so doing prioritize truth over love, or by embracing a kind of universalism, which tends to emphasize love at the expense of truth.

At present we seem to be leaning significantly towards the more conservative end of this spectrum (truth over love) because it appears to be the most expedient method for ordering our collective life and for establishing what is or is not consistent with the received idea of Christian truth. This leads to a tendency to limit and contain Christian truth within rigid interpretations of Scripture and tradition which fail to connect with many people today. It involves using human intelligence in a one-dimensional and rational way, reinforced by a top-down hierarchical and managerial authority structure, so as to prevent 'woolliness'. Employing these methods generally succeeds in preventing compassion from getting in the way of 'management'. In other words, with this approach, compassion and creativity are not allowed to complicate things by softening the edges of policy and decision-making, especially when it comes to resolving disputes. But these rational methods come at a cost. They create winners and losers. By doing so, they inhibit and ultimately stifle the dynamic energy of God's surprising truth which is still 'working' in the life of the Church.

So what if we were to say that in the interest of loving one another more truthfully, as we have been commanded to do, we were to stop worrying about who has got the right truth, concentrating instead on being present together, held in the embrace of the crucified and risen Christ, before the Father? If we were to 'let go' of our own 'truth' accounts, would we be annihilated, literally 'made nothing'? Or might it be possible for us to see our own truth not as absolute, but as only making sense when it is viewed through the eyes of someone whose understanding is quite different from our own?

Perhaps this is what Jesus means when he says that the truth will set us free (John 8.32). It sets us free from ourselves and free to join in God's outworking of the truth in our life of Christian community and in the world. In working together in practical ways because our confidence is based in love for one another, we reveal truth. Here is an example of what I mean by this.

Loving truthfully – Living Water

During my time as Anglican Chaplain at Cardiff University, a group of students, many of whom (but by no means all) were from the Christian Union, decided to do something practical for people coming out of the Student Union after a long night's partying. The clubbers were often well over the limit, badly in need of rehydration and the occasional friendly arm to see them to their front door. The idea was not to evangelize but simply to be there for people, as a mixed group of Christians, listening to their stories and giving practical support in the form of bottles of water, or hot chocolate in colder weather. They also handed out flip-flops to girls wearing dangerously high heels, who might otherwise have had to walk home barefoot in order to avoid the risk of breaking an ankle. The group adopted the policy of not speaking about the Christian faith unless directly asked, so there was no evangelizing agenda. This meant that people were relaxed with the Living Water team and started to talk about themselves and their concerns, which often related to faith and religion. The exercise worked because it was resourced in a love which was deepened and sustained through prayer.

The night began and ended with prayer in our chapel. Praying together anchored the activity in the love of God, linked the team members very closely to one another and made it possible for that shared love to be passed on to those they were serving. Establishing this bond of love also meant that, for a while at least, differences in churchmanship were set aside, which in turn made it easier to form friendships within the

Living Water group itself. These cross-denominational friend-ships were a sign of the truth of God's Spirit at work in the life of the chaplaincy, allowing the chaplaincy to become a sign to the wider university of the deeper truth of the gospel.

Christians within the Living Water group continued to have widely divergent views about certain Christian teachings and ways of worshipping, but the exercise, which still takes place regularly during term time, revealed one overarching truth, which is that irrespective of our differences, we all *love* the same Lord. Love for God became Living Water's shared truth language. It became the truth to which they were called to witness together. All this suggests that truth needs to be 'freed' from being simply a matter of being right or wrong if it is to become the means of freeing others so that they too can experience the truth of God's love.

On freeing the truth

In his conversation with the theologian, Nicodemus, Jesus chides him for trying to manage and define truth in a purely logical, or propositional, way. He wants Nicodemus to use his imagin-ation and allow what Jesus is saying about the need to be reborn in the Spirit to become a free and living truth, capable of liberating people from all the fears and constrictions placed on them by the formal religion of his time. His conversation with Nicodemus suggests that Nicodemus lacks something essential in his life which only a truth freed from the weighty constrictions of the law and of formal religious teaching can give him. It is clear from the conversation that Nicodemus needs to recognize this lack in himself.

When Nicodemus responds to Jesus' words about the need to be reborn by saying that the idea defies logic and therefore cannot be true, he is doing (no doubt unintentionally) what sceptics do today, that is, he is trying to make sense of spiritual truth through mechanistic or logical ways of thinking. Jesus points out that this way of thinking about truth and the Spirit is not only misleading, but wrong. He tells Nicodemus that truth which is of God's Spirit is not to be thought of in purely rational terms, because the Spirit is a dynamic, ongoing and creative movement, the life of God in the energy of his own Spirit at work in the hearts of those who love him and recognize their need for him, and in the work which this love compels them to do in the world. When Jesus says, on another occasion, that he is 'the way, and the truth, and the life' (John 14.6), he is saying that only he himself, the Son of God, can fully meet this need. Recognizing our need for God is a *revelation* of truth.

The truth as it is revealed in Christ now becomes the basis for making sense of our lives and of all the things which matter to us, whether or not these pertain directly to religious faith. The kind of truth Jesus is talking about is the missing piece in the jigsaw which suddenly makes sense of the whole picture.

For the Church as Christian community, the truth as it is revealed in Jesus Christ has a further significance. Christ is the 'home base' which Christians of all denominations inhabit and share. In his book *Fidelity Without Fundamentalism*, Gerard Hughes sees this home base as a shared space in which we make sense of different traditions and faith languages within Christianity.[3] His imagery, using three triangles sharing the same base line, helps us to see Christ as the 'place' we come back to, in prayer and in the concrete realities of everyday life. We meet in his name and share his peace when we pray together, and for one another, and when we meet him in the faces of our fellow human beings, especially the suffering and the marginalized. Christians *experience* the truth as *revealed* in both these contexts.

Reading Scripture in another's language

The idea of a shared base brings us back to the importance of language and of the need to know one another's truth language in order to engage with the truth from other perspectives.[4] It is only by engaging with the truth as other Christians experience it that we can pray with and for them in a meaningful way. Nowhere is this more important than in the context of how we read Scripture.[5]

Christians read Scripture in different ways. Some see in it God's law, given to human beings to be applied to their lives here and now. Others work with the complexities and nuances of Scripture by paying attention to context and to the particular emphasis which the editors and writers of the various books might have wanted to make at the time of writing, but whatever their approach, most find in Scripture a God who invites them into a loving relationship with him. So Scripture is both life-giving and life-preserving for anyone who reads it attentively while also respecting where other readers are coming from in their understanding of truth.

Nevertheless, there are Christians who find such an open approach to the interpretation of Scripture difficult to accept. They feel that to give truth the kind of freedom that I have been talking about is tantamount to *syncretism*, whereby all religions, and any one person's version of biblical truth, are seen to combine into a single truth; or they fear that the truth of Scripture could be corrupted and degenerate into *relativism*, whereby Christian truth is compromised when it is made to 'fit in' with other individually held truths, some religious and some not. The danger, as they see it, is that these different ways of thinking allow individuals to decide for themselves whether or not a particular truth suits them and, on that basis, to believe it or not, which amounts to a kind of 'pick 'n' mix' approach to Christian belief. Many Christians fear that syncretism and relativism might undermine the *absolute* nature of Christian truth as it is revealed in the Bible. But Jesus does not supply any absolute definition of truth, apart from saying that he himself *is* the truth. Even when Pontius Pilate puts the question, 'What is truth?' to him directly, he says nothing (John 18.38).

Truth, love and honour

All this suggests that the kind of truth which is of God, and which is embodied in Jesus, is outside and beyond the realm of what is provable. All we can say is that it is bound up in God's love. Love and truth are inseparable because they are embodied in the person of Jesus. It follows that in the life of the Church, truth can only be worked out or 'proved' in the love Christians have for one another, not in subjective feelings or emotions, but by honouring the Christians we dislike or disagree with in the fullness of their humanity, as brothers and sisters in Christ. By 'honouring' I do not mean simply being nice to them by going through the words and motions of loving them, since that would be a lie and the worst form of betrayal. Honouring other Christians means being confident that they matter deeply to God and that he loves and honours them for who they are, not for being right or wrong about the truth of the Bible or for belonging to the right denomination or churchmanship. So the only way Christians can 'prove' that what they believe in is true is in the way they relate to one another in a hospitality which is modelled by God himself. In the next chapter I shall be looking at some of the ways in which that hospitality can be nurtured and developed.

Questions to reflect on and discuss

- Have you read any books, or seen a painting or sculpture, which point to a truth which is of the Spirit?
- Do you have a particular parable, or passage of Scripture, which conveys a fresh meaning to you every time you read it?
- What do you think Jesus meant when he said, 'The truth will set you free' (John 8.32)?
- In what sense is the Bible true for you?
- What does loving a Christian from a different churchmanship require of you?

5

Radical hospitality

I have just come from a meeting with a clergy colleague. At one point his dog ran in with a partially destroyed feather duster. Chaos ensued and we had to stop the meeting so that my colleague could vacuum up the mess while the rest of us dealt with the coloured feathers stuck to the dog's nose. It was fun. Church people, and clergy especially, are seldom associated with fun. This is odd when we think how often Jesus seems to have had fun in the company of friends.

When I was on retreat a few years ago, someone gave a homily on the subject of whether or not Jesus ever laughed. The preacher concluded that he probably didn't. But a solemn po-faced Jesus seems very much at odds with the Jesus who loved parties and informal social gatherings. He even performed his first miracle to save a wedding reception from disaster. The more profound theological significance of this miracle, that the water became wine and was a foreshadowing of the shedding of Christ's blood for his Church, often obscures the very human circumstances which provoked it in the first place. Running out of wine before the end of the reception would have caused great embarrassment to the parents hosting the wedding and would have brought the party to an end.

The way Jesus responded to this potentially embarrassing situation has a significance of its own. Christ's courtesy, consideration and affection for the young couple and for their parents led him to act before his 'hour' (John 2.4). His action was a sign of the salvation to come because joy and celebration in him are God's ultimate purpose for the human race. God's purpose is not that human beings should be gloomy and serious in his presence but that they should be reconciled to one another and reunited in Christ. They will eventually celebrate that deep unity in the eternal heavenly banquet which is foreshadowed in Christ's ministry and evoked in the Eucharist. I shall say more about the significance of the Eucharist later but for the moment we can think of it as a shared celebration of thanksgiving for our life together in Christ.[1] Jesus came to give us this life in all its fullness, both now and in the hereafter (John 10.10). He did not come to demand an end to the good things which make for living life to the full, or to inhibit the joy Christians experience when they are in fellowship with one another. The life Jesus brings is one of hospitality and celebration.

The whole salvation story is an invitation into fellowship with a Trinitarian God. It turns on the idea of God's infinite hospitality, that he is a God who is always inviting us to belong together within his own joy and relatedness. Rublov's icon of the Trinity expresses this perfectly. It is set in the context of the hospitality shown by Abraham and Sarah to their three angelic visitors (Gen. 18.1–8), but it is really about God's hospitality towards us. In the three angels we see a Trinitarian God who has prepared a meal for us, the Eucharist. The icon anticipates the promise of eternal joy in God's company. We are destined for intimate friendship with God in the fullness of our humanity, which is why the bread is so significant. But the icon has another even deeper significance. We eat when we are hungry, in other words, when we need food in order to stay alive. The bread which is pictured in the icon signifies the satisfying of a human need for reconciliation and fellowship with one another and with God, which is the meaning and purpose of human life.

The hospitality of God

So the miracle at Cana is a foreshadowing of God's greater rescue operation, our redemption worked out through the hospitality of God shown to us in Jesus. Repentance begins in the moment we recognize our need for God for his own sake, because without him our lives will end in futility and shame, as the wedding party would have ended had Jesus not stepped in and rescued it. It is his friends' need which prompts this miracle and it is God's generosity and our need which compel him to live, suffer and die with us, so that we can share in his risen life and feel at home in his company. His humanity embraces our own and allows us to believe and continue to hope in this saving hospitality. In it, he fully identifies with the human condition. His life, as well as his death and resurrection, is worked out in his rejoicing to be one of us.

When someone has reason to rejoice, the normal and healthy human response is to rejoice with that person, or at least to want to rejoice. While negative feelings may sometimes get in the way, most of us are ashamed of such feelings and try to overcome them and rejoice sincerely with the other person. So when Jesus says that he has come to give us life in all its fullness, he is communicating his own joy in being with us, which is why we talk about the 'good news' of the gospel. He is not talking about the kind of false rejoicing which makes you wonder, rather cynically, what people are really thinking when they say, 'I'm so pleased for her.' Nor is he talking about superficial happiness, easily faked for the sake of appearances in order to conform to the expectations of others or to hide from one's own inner woundedness. He is talking about a deep vital joy which brings forth life, a joy which is generous and creative because it adds to the joy of the other person.

We block God's creative joy, his life-giving creativity, when we settle for the things which make for spiritual death, for a happiness which is basically sterile because it is not able to be renewed from within God's love. My vegetable garden is providing me with an excellent illustration of this. It has received quite a battering from recent gale-force winds. Three cabbages which, until yesterday, seemed perfectly healthy have been uprooted and blown away and now lie limply behind the currant bushes. On closer inspection I can see that they have club root. Their wizened little roots are not strong enough to withstand the gales because they have no means to grow, to allow their life to be renewed by the rich earth, so those happy looking cabbages will never deliver what they promised.

Resourcing joy

Happiness does not always deliver what it promises. If it did, why would we need to go on striving for it for all our working lives? And why would we spend our remaining years coming to terms with regret – regret for what has not been achieved, or for what achievement and success have cost us personally, especially in the context of our relationships? We spend much of our lives striving for what the world gives, for success of one kind or another, because we dread failure. Failure makes us feel 'invisible', as if we no longer existed.

John, who was made redundant at a time when he least expected it, described how he felt when he was told the news: 'When I was called in to my line manager's office, my mind was elsewhere, thinking about the work I was in the middle of doing and which he'd interrupted, wanting to get back to it as soon as possible. Then out of the blue, he just told me that they were having to cut costs. I was still only half listening, until he said something about a redundancy package. Then it started to hit me. I used to work from home some of the time. It took weeks to get used to not receiving emails or phone calls. I felt completely cut off from everything and everyone. I felt they were avoiding me. It was like someone had died. But it was me who'd died in a way. I just felt as if I'd been written off the register of the living.' Fear, especially fear of failure, cuts us off from life because it cuts us off from other people.

Churches can also be driven by an underlying fear of failure, the fear that they too will be 'written off the register of the living'.

Many clergy are dogged by anxiety and by a bureaucracy which presents them with very secular criteria for success without resourcing them spiritually through individual mentoring and ordinary human friendship. Churches and their clergy run out of joy when the source of that joy runs dry. In other words, the politics of success take over where Christian collegiality, what St Paul calls genuine love (Rom. 12.9), ceases to exist. So churches fear failure and yearn to be successful. But where trust is blocked by fear of failure, clergy and people find themselves in a life-denying or sterile situation, one in which a church becomes bogged down in administration and mission action plans and eventually grinds to a halt in its journey towards God. As a result its internal relationships suffer.

This grinding to a halt is like a car stalling, or one which won't start on a cold morning. In the days when chokes were part of a car's starting mechanism, revving the accelerator and overdoing the choke was sure to flood the engine, so the only solution was to wait. Perhaps Christians try too hard in the wrong way. We overdo the choke by organizing events and conferences and by activities which aim at togetherness and productivity but leave little time for waiting, for the silence and space needed for truthful conversations to happen, the kinds of conversations which might allow Christians to connect with one another at a deeper level.

All this suggests that things need to happen a little more gently if our hearts are to 'get started' again. Perhaps we need to 'just sit there' rather than 'do something', so that uninhibited joy can flow from God's Spirit into our life of Christian community, our shared life of the spirit which is a life of hospitable prayer.

Hospitable prayer

We made a deliberate decision to make hospitable prayer a reality in the life of the chaplaincy. One of our students approached me during Freshers' Week saying that she had sensed an urgent need for a period of uninterrupted prayer in our chapel. So a few weeks later we held a 24/7 prayer vigil. The chapel was open for seven days and nights for uninterrupted prayer. People signed up to one-hour slots throughout the seven-day period and those which could not be filled during daytime hours, because students had lectures to attend, were filled by a Catholic sister from a nearby convent.

The 24/7 exercise had long-lasting and wide-ranging effects. It signalled to the university that the chapel was primarily a place of prayer and that all were welcome to use it. It strengthened and gave confidence to those who already used the chaplaincy and by being grounded in *a shared love for Christ* it created deeper understanding between students of different church backgrounds. Everyone experienced that love together in the hospitable silence of prayer. The confidence acquired by relaxing together in silent prayer and by a shared service of celebration at the end of the week established a sense of real commonality from which the Living Water project was later born. It also gave rise to a quiet and confident joy and an enduring sense of the presence of Christ in that building. Many who came to the chaplaincy for the first time remarked on the 'good feeling' they experienced as they stepped through the front door.[2]

The 24/7 experience also revealed that prayer grounded in a positive desire for reconciliation has a way of getting into everything and generating joy. The silence gave people permission not to have to try too hard to make things work, one of the besetting problems of most initial church gatherings. Things simply worked because we were focused on Christ and were aware of others present in the chapel without feeling anxious or burdened by them. This sense of a shared purpose (remaining focused on Christ) generated trust and allowed joy to simply happen in a quiet and unobtrusive way. In other words, we shared Christ's peace at the deepest level of our common life.

I later found myself wondering why it is that people seldom experience such a sense of deep joy in the context of Sunday church services. Things are either solemn, or happy in a rather forced way, and this sits uncomfortably with the real meaning and purpose of worshipping together, especially in the context of the Eucharist. Think, for example, of the way the Peace is exchanged in certain churches in the UK.[3] People are either in a hurry to get through the whole business as quickly as possible so that they can get back to their private time with God, or basking in a collective euphoria, or they are looking over the shoulder of the person they are greeting to see if there is anyone more interesting or important who they should acknowledge in the brief amount of time allowed. The gesture has nothing to do with sharing the peace and joy of Christ. In fact it does not involve sharing at all because meaningful exchange is impossible when no one makes eye contact. We get the same effect in churches with an enthusiastic welcome team at the door but where newcomers are often ignored during the service, as well as during coffee afterwards.

Celebration and fellowship: crossing the Catholic–Protestant divide

In the context of the Eucharist, the exchange of the Peace comes just before the offertory prayers. The Peace emphasizes the hospitality of the Eucharist and links the ministry of the word to that of the sacrament. Despite the differences which exist between Christians over what actually takes place in the moment of consecration, the Eucharist that follows, known also as Holy Communion or Mass, bridges the Protestant–Catholic divide. In sharing the Peace the whole worshipping community takes responsibility for maintaining that bridge, the gesture itself drawing our humanity and our human affections into the love of God. It is a sign of our acceptance of God's hospitality, a forward movement *towards* other Christians and *into* deeper fellowship *in* Christ. When we say, 'Peace be with you', we are giving voice to the fellowship we all share in Christ. The Peace brings together and involves everyone in what has been done up to that moment and in what we are about to witness together, the presence of Christ in our midst. So it is a kind of living expectation of the kingdom of heaven in the present moment, the 'already but not quite yet'.[4]

How we think about the Eucharist, and about Christ's presence in that context, will be conditioned to some extent by churchmanship or by our individual faith journeys. I am an Anglican but I received my faith from the Catholic Church in which I grew up. To me, the Eucharist signifies the hospitable and enduring love of God as well as his presence. In it, I rejoice and am thankful for God's unconditional love and for the hospitality shown to me by the Anglican Church. But no matter how we think about presence in connection with the Eucharist it is, as Calvin argued, the people's expectation of Emmanuel, God in our midst, and their love for one another, which make that presence 'real'. Calvin's thinking on the sacraments, and on the Eucharist in particular, was far more reconciliatory than many Christians realize.[5] It is not that Christ's presence has to be summoned up from the collective psyche, but that he is the host inviting us, his guests, to be present to him, as he is present to us. So the Eucharist is a spiritual reality which connects the Church with the world. It is also a foretaste of the heavenly party promised in the future, which is why we speak of *celebrating* the Eucharist.

Celebrating the Eucharist involves eating and drinking. In one sense, that is what makes this celebration sacramental.[6] It has to do with physical matter, and with recognizing the reality of Jesus' presence with us in the breaking of the bread, as he was recognized by the disciples who ate with him at Emmaus after the resurrection. This reality, which has to do with the physical and human business of preparing a meal, is what also makes for fellowship, so the members of a church or Christian community only become community in the fullest sense when they worship and eat together. But fellowship does not have to be grounded in a formal eucharistic meal, with liturgy and a celebrant. An ordinary meal, or even coffee and biscuits, links the spiritual with the physical and makes the spiritual a little less intimidating.

Any tangible reminder of God's presence among us will also be a reminder of the fellowship which exists between different Christians. Before I was ordained we used to hold an agape once a month in our house. An agape is a simple sharing of bread and wine without the words of consecration. After the agape we would have supper with some good wine. Everyone brought food. In fact it became quite a gastronomic event. It was a supper party with something extra, the peace and joy of the risen Christ in our midst. The laughter and conversation were preceded by grace sung in three parts and the evening usually ended, for some reason, with the singing of 'On Ilkley Moor Baht 'At'. The whole event felt like a prelude to the heavenly banquet foretold in Scripture. It was a communion of saints, with Christ present to everyone around that table, and in the faces of the children, who were an integral part of the event.

Children did not have separate arrangements made for them because this would have created a sense of difference, of adult superiority. Instead, we celebrated their special significance by asking the youngest person to carry the little oil lamp[7] from the room in which the agape had taken place to the kitchen where the meal was to be. He or she would then light the candles on the table from the oil lamp, using a taper and watched over by the person putting the final touches to the meal, before announcing that supper was ready and leading everyone to the table. This connected the agape meal with supper. The youngest person fulfilled the most important 'priestly' duty by linking the two aspects of the celebration, the agape and the meal, and also reminded us of the prophecy of

Isaiah that God's people would be led in humility by a little child (Isa. 11.6).

Radical acceptance and surprise

We learned from the agape that God accepts us as *we* are and at the same time remains true to himself as *he* is. He accepts us by the courteous offer of his divine hospitality and he invites us to accept one another in the same way, by seeking out the goodness in one another, as he sees the goodness in us. This is the essence of good hospitality, and good hospitality can yield surprising results.

A friend of mine suffers from depression, along with the low self-esteem which depression invariably brings with it. She described a phone call she received from a relative who she found particularly undermining and difficult. The conversation took a turn which suddenly revealed the goodness of that person, a goodness which my friend had never noticed before because her defences were always up when he was around. In the moment of recognizing his hidden goodness, she rediscovered a little of her own. Seeing the good in the other allows us to see the good in ourselves. It inspires confidence, generates trust and leads to the radical acceptance which comes with reconciliation. Radical acceptance forms the basis of hospitable prayer.

Hospitable prayer is a two-way activity established through deeper understanding of a person or situation. It is grounded in silence. In it, we pay attention to God's acceptance of us as we are and we accept others as they are. Hospitable prayer involves deep listening, the kind of listening in which we expect to experience God's presence. We experience it in the silence itself and again later, when those who have been praying silently together begin to engage in discussions or activities. This happened in the context of the work done by Living Water and in the many conversations between young people of different denominations and nationalities at Taizé. Silence also becomes a fertile ground in which to cultivate a deep knowledge of God. The intellect, that part of us which forms opinions and makes judgements about God and about people and situations, is resourced from this deep inner space, privately and in the context of community. Nowhere is this truer than in the way we read Scripture together.

Reading Scripture together – deep listening

Experiencing God's presence when reading Scripture together requires reading from a place of deep listening. In this silent place we are both individually and collectively vulnerable to God. We can love him unreservedly because we do so in silence, so there is no need to be worried about what others will think. Silence and deep listening create a safe space in which we can be vulnerable to one another. Being vulnerable in silence allows us to be surprised by the goodness of those around us and by their unique understanding of truth, the truth which is revealed to us as part of that goodness. So being silent together in God's presence generates trust. Once trust has been established, we can let go of the truth as we see it in any given passage and allow the words to speak to us in new ways.

We tried this exercise at the end of the 24/7 week, with a Catholic student leading us. He used two tried and tested methods for reading Scripture out of a time of shared silence. The first, known as *lectio divina*, involves 'savouring' the text. It works best with psalms or books of the Bible which either address God directly or speak about him. The psalms, the book of Job and the Song of Songs, along with the farewell discourses and Jesus' prayer for his disciples in St John's Gospel (John 13.31—17.26) are particularly suited to this method. We do *lectio divina* in such a way as to allow the text, or a few words from Scripture, to soak into our inner consciousness, as water soaks into dry earth, so that the words penetrate every moment of our waking day. They remain with us, just below the surface of active conscious thought.

Here is a basic 'method' for doing *lectio divina*: read the text through slowly, taking no more than a couple of verses, or what is needed for the passage to make sense. Savour the words as if you were enjoying a glass of good wine or the most delicate sorbet. Without thinking too hard about what it means, allow the text to work itself into your imagination. Just let the words draw you into God.

This is not about mental concentration. It is about deep inner attentiveness, fixing one's centre and one's whole being on God while we savour the words of the text. If you can learn some of the words by heart, so much the better. Eventually, these words of Scripture will become your mantra, part of your breathing. They will attune themselves to the rhythm of your body and shape themselves around all that happens in your day. This is how we experience God's word as a living force, a lifeblood within us. When we do this exercise as a group, we take this experience of having been vulnerable to God into our prayer together and across our churchmanship boundaries. It changes the way we go on thinking about the Church and the part we have to play in it as members of a diverse but single body.

Another deep listening method for reading Scripture involves imagining yourself into the situation you are reading about. This is best suited to stories, or moments when Jesus is in conversation with someone – with one of the disciples or with the Samaritan woman, for example. With this method, we take the place of the person who is engaging with Jesus, or imagine ourselves just being there as a bystander or as another person in the story. The important thing is to be present to the situation and allow the words spoken by Jesus, or by another person, to speak into our own hearts and to connect with our own experience. When this exercise is done in a group, someone should read the passage slowly, repeating phrases if necessary, so that we know that we are all focusing on the same moment together. This method of listening to the word of God is not only an aid to concentration but, more importantly, it allows Scripture to connect us more deeply with one another. It builds up our common life from within the life of God's Spirit.

Both these methods allow different Christians to be hospitable to one another from within the hospitality of God. In being present to him together, in reading and 'inwardly digesting'[8] the words of Scripture, and also in welcoming Christ in their midst at the Eucharist, they experience his presence. This deep encounter with Christ and with one another is what Christ promised would happen when two or more are gathered together in his name (Matt. 18.20). Deep listening to Scripture makes Scripture sacramental. It has the power to transform and, with the Eucharist, becomes the means for reconciliation between Christians. In the next chapter I shall be looking at how reconciliation at this deeper level might lead Christians into the kind of holiness which makes the good news of the gospel something to celebrate in the world today.

Things to try out or think about

- When did you last attend a wedding? Use the memory of this wedding as the basis for imagining yourself into what happened at Cana. What would Jesus look like at the wedding you attended? What kind of clothes would he be wearing? Would he be a close relative? Who were his friends? Build up a picture of the situation so that it becomes real to you. You can do this as a group or individually.
- Does your church use silence in its worship? If not, what would be people's response if you tried it one day – possibly without advance warning?
- How does your church pray about its outreach activities? Do you pray with other Christians? Have you thought of holding a joint service with a church which worships in a

way which is quite different from your own? If you find the idea off-putting, ask people from the other church how they feel about it. What can you do to learn more about why the other church worships in the way it does?

- Is diversity potentially enriching or divisive?

6

Reconnecting with holiness

How can Christians be holy in a way which inspires confidence in the message of the gospel and attracts others to Christ? Jean was one such person. She quietly assumed the job of secretary of the PCC, as well as her official role of treasurer. Jean was unselfishly competent. Being competent relieves others of anxiety, contributes to the smooth running of any enterprise, large or small, and makes for better working relationships. Competence with good-humoured kindness inspires trust. Being wilfully incompetent has the reverse effect. Jean was also the person who could be relied upon to produce coffee, biscuits and home-made marmalade (on sale at a modest price with proceeds going to the church) after the Sunday Eucharist. Jean had something about her which was extra, something outside the ordinary. When she handed you a cup of coffee you felt you had connected with Christ.

During the 1980s, at the time of the Greenham Common Women's Peace Camp, Mary, who had been there for a number of weeks, told a friend that she was looking for 'a bit of spirituality'. She wanted to renew her sense of purpose by strengthening the connection between what she and others were doing at Greenham and the whole meaning and purpose of being human. Perhaps, without realizing it at first, she was looking for a way to connect with God. She wanted to place what she was doing within his will and purpose for future generations. She may have sensed that she was already doing this but she needed 'a bit of spirituality' to make her intuition real. She wanted to give it substance, to know that she was in relationship with the one who was the source of the love and energy which went into her work for peace.

There are many holy people like Jean and Mary. They are holy not only because of what they do, but because of who they are. Such people do not think about being holy, or about how they should come across to others. They are simply vulnerable to God and aware of their need of him. This frees them from the kinds of needs and longings which take up so much of our time and emotional energy. It allows them to work with God for others and to take on jobs which seem tedious, unimportant or downright dangerous. Holy people hold society together because they know what it means to love and be loved by God. They also have the right priorities. They know what matters in life.

Challenging situations, ones which challenge our ability to survive, lead us to focus on the things which matter most to us. Mary wanted to reconnect at a deeper level with the meaning and purpose of what she was doing. Her remark reveals a yearning for God, a yearning for holiness. It is this innate desire for holiness, experienced as the ultimate 'making sense' of life, which drives a person's desire for change, for seeing an end to the politics of war and the beginning of lasting peace and healing.

Holiness camouflaged

Holiness has a kind of magnetic appeal. Holy people are attractive, often despite appearances. In spite of his rather gruff manner and unkempt appearance, the 'whisky priest' in Graham Greene's *The Power and the Glory* was loved by the men and women hiding from the police because they sensed that he loved them, and that he was prepared to give them everything he had, including his life. He did not look or sound like a priest but he brought Christ to others in a very immediate way.

Some of the most gifted poets and composers have been far from amiable in private. These people are attractive at a different level. By being who they are in the context of whatever work they do, they draw others towards God. By signalling that life has a purpose beyond the material, beyond the superficial and boring, they make others stop and ask themselves what they are doing with their lives. Holy people are seldom bored and never boring. Like Jean, they will resist boredom by being fully engaged and creative in whatever they are doing in the present moment. The practical business at hand will be resourced from an energy which comes from God. They show others how to reconnect with God because that is where their own goodness is resourced.

In all this, they will also have known suffering. Reconnecting with God often begins when we are at a low point in our lives. It obliges us to come to terms with failure and brokenness. When this happens, we literally 'make sense' of our lives by allowing them to come into focus through memory and in a conscious desire to turn back into God. This turning back into God involves both mind and heart. It obliges us to re-examine our social and political priorities, as well as our personal priorities, in an objective and a subjective way, bringing the two together wherever possible.

Prophetic holiness

Change of mind and heart entails rethinking the needs and desires which define us, both individually and as a society. At Greenham Common, Mary was defining herself and those who were with her as people whose priorities lay with the survival of the world, for the sake of future generations, and with a prophetic need to call to account those with military and economic power. Her holiness drew her into community with others, many of whom were not Christians but whose shared priorities made them a holy community in God's sight. They were holy because they cared about righteousness. They were taking a stand against governments who allow concern for righteousness to be sidelined in favour of expediency presented in terms of 'values'.[1]

Jesus speaks of judgement as a basic separation of those who care about the needs and suffering of others from those who do not. In his parable of the last judgement (Matt. 25.31–46), Jesus says that the goats, like the rich man who ignored the beggar outside his own front door (Luke 16.19–31), are those who are indifferent to the needs of others, who neither notice nor care about what is going on around them. If Jesus were telling this story today, he might point to the sinful economic and political systems which his followers could influence or change. Holiness involves having certain priorities. It also brings responsibility. Responsibility anchors well-meaning altruistic thoughts in the realities of society in a desire to protect and enhance life.

The Greenham women were challenging powerful nations to rethink their priorities with regard to the development and use of nuclear warheads, so they were witnessing to the vital connection which exists between what is done politically and socially and the enlivening force of God's Spirit. The Holy Spirit was working through the women themselves. It was their presence, and the physical hardship which they chose to endure as a prophetic community, which convicted those with political and military strength to change their minds, using the words of the Greenham manifesto itself, about nuclear weapons.[2] For Christians involved in the Campaign for Nuclear Disarmament (CND), and in any other form of prophetic witness, the meaning and purpose of right priorities leading to prophetic actions is shaped and resourced from within a still greater purpose, the visible outworking of God's love for humanity in the world of today.

Being a prophetic community

Christians are given the prophetic task of making this out-working visible, beginning from within the life of the Christian community itself, so reconciliation is the most urgent and immediate task facing the Church today. People outside the Church are hoping, in the fullest sense of the word, to see Christians pray together, think together and work together. They are hoping for a more compassionate Church, one which has learned through suffering. Trying to order a divided Church which has not first addressed its own woundedness is proving to be a futile exercise.[3] We become more, rather than less, polarized. We try to hide from our disunity by an increasing politicization of our common life and by keeping generally busy. As a result, we create the impression that we have given up altogether on reconciliation.

Busyness is a good thing insofar as it allows us to focus on practical witness. Engaging creatively with its locality focuses and lends credibility to a community's shared faith and, as we found with Living Water, builds friendships and strengthens community life, but it is also physically, emotionally and spiritually demanding. It needs 'in-reach' to sustain it. Without a shared life of prayer, and regular periods of prayerful silence undertaken together, practical and physical witness consumes all our available energy and personal resources. Periods of silence give pause for thought. They forestall unwise remarks, prevent hasty decisions, and allow for a certain amount of physical recharging.

I experienced the way silence recharges people in a very immediate way when I was chaplain to the Student Cross pilgrimage in 2008. Student Cross is organized by university students. It was started in 1948 by a group of Catholic and Anglican students who wanted to witness together to the meaning of the cross and to the Easter experience itself.[4] Students, and others, walk from one of several locations, known as 'legs', for all or part of Holy Week. On Holy Saturday, they meet in Walsingham, having walked ten to fifteen miles a day for three to five days, sleeping on church hall floors at night, and taking turns to carry a large cross. They carry the cross in groups of three, two at the front and one supporting the vertical beam. They feel the physical weight of the cross as something which holds them together, a shared burden which is heavy and hard but in which they experience being community in the deepest sense. As they walk, they talk, pray and occasionally sing. They also have periods of silence which give substance to the prayers and conversations and which reinforce a particular kind of friendship in community, a deeper unity, which attracts others to Christ.

The challenge to change

I found that the silence allowed the cross to speak for itself into the hearts of those walking, as well as to the residents of the villages and small towns we passed through. During these periods of silence, people came out of their houses, and occasionally joined us as we walked. The silence reinforced the collective will and the desire to witness truthfully to the reality of the cross, to what it signifies for today. This meant that we had to work at understanding and hearing one another's truth, and learn to respect one another in the way we prayed and talked and even in what we sang. We had to learn to hear the truth in new ways, leaning into the cross in order to do so and finding in it the means for change and renewal.

Student Cross reflects the pilgrim way of life to which the Church is called. Christians are called to move on and to change while remaining centred on the cross, which they carry together. Like those taking part in Student Cross, we lean into the cross as we move from familiar ways of thinking and practising the faith into the unfamiliar and different, but we are still carrying the same cross and loving the same Lord.

The cross draws Christians together but it also burdens us with certain responsibilities. It invites us to question whether a particular churchmanship or local church is still right for us, or has become like an old wineskin, too brittle and unyielding to accommodate new ideas and ways of encountering a vital and living God. In the parable of the wineskins (Luke 5.37–39),[5] Jesus tells his listeners that nobody would think of putting fresh new wine into old wineskins because the fermentation process has not finished and the old wineskins, which have lost their elasticity, will burst when the wine starts to mature. New wine goes into new skins so that both can expand together. He is not saying that the old skins were no good to begin with, but that they have served their purpose and that it would be a bad idea to use them a second time round. Our own faith formation and maturing process works along similar lines. We may begin in one place, or have come to faith through a particular church context, but as faith matures through prayer, reflection and life experience, it can sometimes be difficult to contain it in the old church context. It may be time to move on.

Moving on can be difficult and painful. For one thing, those leaving a church or fellowship will often be resented or misunderstood because they are acting prophetically. Prophecy involves being obedient to the Holy Spirit and witnessing, through the choices we make and the words we speak, to the ongoing creative force of God's love at work in our lives. It tends to stir things up because it faces us with the need for change and with our responsibility to live with integrity by being honest with ourselves, and by living truthfully. Christians are called to grow and change so that they can be the means of growth and change for others. They do not move across churchmanship boundaries just because they fancy something different. They move because they must. They are compelled to do so by God's Holy Spirit so that they can grow in the kind of holiness which will enable them to continue to witness truthfully to the gospel.

Connecting through worship

This brings us back to the question of what it is that people who are looking to reconnect with their faith, or who are coming to Christianity for the first time, really expect from the Church. What does it have to offer them? Mary, the woman at Greenham Common who was searching for 'spirituality', needed something more than a means of escape from the harsh conditions of the Women's Peace Camp. She was not looking for something which would help her to imagine herself out of her situation, or even give it a 'spiritual' focus. She was looking for a way to connect what she was doing with a holy God who shapes and gives meaning and purpose to prophetic action. She wanted a living relationship with this God.

People who pass by our churches, or who visit once or twice but never return, are looking for the same thing. They are looking for a more meaningful spiritual life, one which connects them with God, so that they can experience him, and so that he can work his purpose in their lives. In other words, they are looking for holiness. But they often find that the people inside the churches they visit are either too busy, too noisy, or too taken up with the minutiae of their own internal problems to be able to help them. This general sense of busyness and superficial purpose makes newcomers feel excluded, something which is only made worse if no one has engaged with them in genuine conversation, however brief, before the service begins. If someone coming from a different worship background is not greeted or welcomed when arriving, then the sense of isolation will only increase, and this will impoverish the newcomer's worship. We need to establish genuine fellowship with those around us if worship, whether formal or informal, is to 'work' in the fullest sense.

Some evangelical churches make a point of asking everyone to exchange a few words with their immediate neighbour before the start of the service. It relaxes people and can be of great help to the worship itself. But it can also make the church feel chatty and cause the service to get off to a rather unfocused start. This can be especially problematic for churches or services which have no formal liturgy to return to once the exchange of greetings has ended. It is difficult to move seamlessly from socializing to worship and can be particularly challenging for the person leading. He or she will have to work hard to get everyone's attention but not in such a way that the focus remains fixed on the worship leader rather than on God. The church where I served my curacy always had a short period of silence immediately before the start of the service, once the choir were inside the main door. It signalled the end to socializing and the beginning of worship by allowing the congregation, the choir and whoever was leading the service to be properly centred on God from the beginning.

Worship works for the newcomer when that person begins to feel confident whatever the context. Ideally, we should feel as comfortable in someone else's denominational setting as we do in our own. This only happens when we have engaged with people as fellow human beings, rather than as evangelicals, Methodists, or Anglo-Catholics. These different ways of being church are important insofar as they provide a family context in which to mature and grow in the faith, but when they become closed or prescriptive they make it difficult to relate in a relaxed way across the denominational boundaries. This in turn makes worship feel closed and alienating. Part of the difficulty may lie with the theology which informs a church's particular truth language, and with which we may not readily identify. So we will need to make some effort to understand its truth language by trusting those around us enough to allow them into our own inner space. This is the kind of radical hospitality I described in the last chapter. It involves holding the people worshipping around us in the love of God and within God's own inner life.

Here it might be helpful to return to the story of the prodigal and take the place of the elder son. He felt alienated from the rest of the family, especially from his father and brother. Worshipping in a different church environment can feel alienating because in-built negative feelings have a way of resurfacing when we make ourselves vulnerable to one another in the context of worship. The elder brother would have had to wrestle with a complicated set of reactions and conflicting emotions. He might have felt bitterness and envy on the one hand, and pity on the other. Perhaps he could not quite come to terms with the fact that he loved his wayward sibling.

Worshipping alongside other Christians can make us suddenly aware of how much we love them, because grace has made us perceive them differently. Grace removes whatever blinkers we are wearing, which distort our vision of God and of our neighbour. This can be disorientating at first, so it is tempting to put the blinkers (or the clever sunglasses which don't allow people to see the wearer's eyes) back on as quickly as possible. But in perceiving our fellow worshippers differently we also catch glimpses of God revealing himself in new and surprising ways. Watching the father embrace his younger brother with such warmth and tenderness revealed something to the elder brother about the abundance of the father's love, and its absolute sincerity and integrity. The elder brother was being given an opportunity to see, in both his father and his younger brother, things he had never seen before.

Our perceptions of other Christians can change. As a result, we find ourselves together with them in an altogether new socio-spiritual environment. By socio-spiritual environment I mean a new orientation towards a particular person, which in turn informs how we relate to others around them as together we love and worship the same holy God. Good worship is therefore social in the fullest sense. It connects us to God and it reinforces our deep connection with one another within God's holiness.

Connecting worship with life

Being connected with one another in God also connects us with the wider community. Reflection on CND and other peace and justice movements suggests that holiness combines two aspects of Christian witness, the external and the internal. The external pertains to the kind of outreach in which everyone works together for the good of the local or global community. The internal pertains to the Christian community's love for God expressed in worship and in love for one another. These two facets of our common life inform and resource each other. Believing that one is more important than the other creates a Martha and Mary situation.

When Jesus told Martha that Mary had chosen the better part (Luke 10.42), he was not saying that spirituality takes precedence over action, but that Martha was missing out on something important at that particular moment. It was a question of timing. Later, after the death of their brother, Lazarus, it would be Martha who would go out to meet Jesus before returning to fetch her sister, who had stayed at home. Martha and Mary represent the external and the internal which, if separated, create further layers of distortion and division in the Church's relationships and in the way it orders its life.

In being denied its inner source of renewal, the external is reduced to what Daniel Hardy calls the 'extrinsic' which, roughly translated, means a preoccupation with the superficial, with data, management strategy and growth statistics.[6] While these concerns appear to justify our existence and make us feel 'relevant' in a secular society, in reality they do the opposite because they leave no time for what Hardy calls the 'intrinsic', the kind of confident waiting on God which a spiritually healthy community ought to be doing. It is within the 'intrinsic' that the Christian community is formed as a genuinely social body which derives the meaning and purpose for its life from within the holiness of God. In being disconnected from the intrinsic, we literally lose the plot. We become disorientated and confused about why we do the things we do and where we should be heading. The same thing happens in reverse. When all a church has to offer is an oasis of spirituality, it gives the impression that it does not want to be disturbed by the realities of life.

Separating the external from the internal reinforces insularity, so we find ourselves once again in a Tonto-like situation. The spiritual life, which ought to drive us towards one another, keeps each group to itself, facing the wall and thinking its own thoughts, instead of moving to the edge of their separate comfort zones, so that the two groups can meet each other in the centre of the room and then go out to meet others wherever they happen to be on their faith journeys.

Living on the edge

The prophetic work of holiness consists in being able to meet people where they are, to be 'God bearers' into every kind of situation. The Orthodox Church describes Mary, the mother of Jesus, as the *theotokos*, the God bearer. She represents all those who carry Christ within them and who allow others to meet him by simply being who they are. They bear God to others all the time, without thinking about it. They also meet him in those same people and in the situations in which they find themselves. They meet him on the edge of life, wherever people are marginalized, and they meet him in their own inner struggle to make sense of God for themselves. In order to bear God to others, and to encounter holiness for ourselves, we have to travel to what William Countryman calls the border country.[7]

A televised serial of the Passion shows Christ suffering and dying 'on the edge', in the border country among the poor and undervalued of Port Talbot, once the steel capital of South Wales.[8] In this Passion play we see a God who is intimately involved with marginalized communities and individuals. Holiness comes through in memories. Christ's suffering and grace are in the man who grieves for the loss of his neighbourhood, which disappeared during the construction of the M4. The motorway slammed its way through Llewellyn Street, removing half the street and destroying in a matter of days a community built up over three generations. Holiness emerges as God makes his presence felt in the bleakness of Port Talbot's streets, in closed shops and businesses and on the anonymous Golgotha of a traffic roundabout. Holiness breaks through into the ordinariness of these things – and this is what is so shocking about the cross itself. The death of Christ brings the 'pure' into everything that is 'impure'. In fact it obliges us to embrace the 'impure', the unholy, if we are to be holy ourselves.

This brings us back to relationships between Christians and to how underlying preoccupations with purity get in the way of holiness in the life of Christian community. Christians who we don't understand become strange to us. They are not really Christians because they are not holy in the way *we* understand holiness. So like Tonto the dog, who turned his face to the wall when he didn't want to be seen, we choose not to 'see' them. They are strange to us because they seem 'unsound', or else 'fundamentalist' and naive, or 'happy clappy' with no sense of tradition, or they come across as 'ritualistic' and so are presumed to be insincere. Each group disparages and distrusts the other. So it becomes imperative, both for the life of the individual and also for the life of the whole Christian community, to keep moving outwards, intellectually as well as spiritually, to keep testing and questioning our reasons and motives for certain gut responses in relation to other Christians and to the issues which divide us at the moment. Jesus upset a great many right-thinking religious people because he pushed the borders of conventional holiness further and further out so that more and more people could be counted as holy in the sight of the Father. Christians are called to do likewise.

Questions to reflect on and discuss

- Do you know any holy people? What is it that makes them holy?
- What does the word 'spirituality' mean to you?
- If asked, how would you go about helping someone 'make sense' of their life?
- Is there a difference between 'morality', in the way CND sees it, and 'values', and if so, what is that difference?
- What, for you, is the difference between the external, or 'extrinsic', and the internal, or 'intrinsic'? Should the two be kept separate?
- Do you ever make a point of worshipping in a church of a different denomination? What do you most enjoy about this? What do you least enjoy?
- What do you think people who are changing churchmanships or denominations are really looking for?
- What do you think those who are looking to return to their faith are hoping to find in a church or fellowship?

7

Reconnecting with Wisdom – thinking and practising the love of God

———————

The God Delusion is a prophetic book because it obliges Christians to re-examine their faith and what keeps it alive. Richard Dawkins claims that people of faith, and not just Christians, have a psychological need which only religion can satisfy.[1] Generally speaking, he accuses them of being intellectually weak. According to Dawkins, religion functions as a sort of 'filler'. It fills the gap left by an inadequate education or by psychological abuse experienced in childhood.[2] But the book is flawed, not only because of what it says, but because of the way it says it. The negative emotion polarizes the argument, so it does not encourage good conversation. Furthermore, the book has also embarrassed and antagonized other atheists.[3]

The God Delusion is an angry book. There is a hurt defensiveness about it. One senses, as so often happens with those who are angry about religion, that their own faith experience, or that of someone close to them, has hurt them and that the pain has never healed. It is still there, just beneath the surface of the diatribe. It seems that the writer is trying to make sense of the pain, to understand it, so he resolves it intellectually by attacking its cause because that is the only option open to him. This potent mixture of anger, pain and fear puts both the writer and the reader in a defensive position. There are also a number of theological threads which need to be untangled. Many of these lead to a basic misunderstanding of belief in relation to faith and of the real meaning and purpose of religion. These muddled ideas give the impression that religion is altogether a bad thing.

Nevertheless, the book serves a prophetic purpose because it invites Christians to check out, and possibly update, their thinking about God and about one another. While it may not be essential to grapple with its theological complexities in detail, Christians do need to think through their faith, and the way it affects their relationships, if they are to grow in holiness. They need to be sure that their need for God is the right kind of need and that their religion remains healthy and, in this sense, a good thing.

The word 'religion' stems from the Latin *ligare*, meaning 'to bind together'. Good religion binds people to God in a healthy way and is reflected in the way it binds people together, in the kind of sociality it creates. How people who follow a certain religion behave towards each other, and towards others, will indicate the extent to which that religion is healthy, at least in terms of how its teachings are put into practice. When people are bound to a religion for its own sake it ceases to be a good religion. It becomes something which they can use for purely human purposes. Religion becomes bad when it is manipulated to suit the needs of the individual, or of a self-interested group who then bind their religion to their political or psychological needs. This deflects religion from its proper course and the religion becomes more important than the spirit of what it teaches. It binds people to itself instead of freeing them into God.

Unbinding religion

There are a number of occasions in the Gospels where we read of Jesus unbinding people, most notably Lazarus, who was unloosed from his grave clothes and from the ultimate binding of death, a prefiguring of Jesus' own triumph over death. Jesus also released people from their 'demons', their *daimonia*. Today, the particular demons which Jesus was addressing are recognized as physical and psychological disorders which can be cured with drugs. But there are other kinds of demons which bind people, most notably the actions and attitudes which cling to us and destroy us from within, and these can lead to addiction to drugs, alcohol, work and violence. These addictions become our way of 'coping' with our destructive 'demons', the demons which bind us.

When our religion becomes a 'coping' mechanism, it no longer has the power to free us from the habits and thoughts which 'bind', and which can even destroy us, because it lacks the loving and creative vitality which only God can give. Coping mechanisms do not enable people to take responsibility for themselves in a way which builds them up as persons because they do not of themselves have the power to generate love. Religion becomes a coping mechanism when it reduces faith to a mechanistic way of addressing the moral and spiritual complexities we encounter in the world we live in today. Faith becomes formulaic, a matter of ticking certain boxes in order that we may be considered Christians or bona fide members of any one Christian group. Ticking boxes and coping with life with the help of religion leaves little time or energy for being simply and silently open to the love of God in Christ, the love which makes religion a source of life and hope and which ought to shape our Christian identity.

When religion parts company with love it destroys people. The desire to destroy ourselves, or other people and the world around us, is what we call sin. If left to itself, sin will overwhelm and bind a person's true self. Sin can also overwhelm nations and religions, or a particular group within either of these two areas of human experience, and history has shown how toxic religion and nationhood become when they are combined. Nationhood and religion tell us who we are in relation to history, to other people and to God. Good religion will help a person shape her life in a way which is meaningful within the social context of a nation and in individual relationships which are shaped through family, friendships and work. Bad religion will do the opposite. It will bind a person to herself by allowing negative feelings to dominate the way she thinks about herself and, as a result, will create an ever widening gap between that person and the rest of society. In other words, she will become alienated. She will live in a way which is more and more defensive because she can neither trust others nor believe in herself as unique and valuable in the eyes of a loving God who has a purpose for her life.

This inbuilt defensiveness binds a person's spirit, so that he cannot reach out for God or to other people. With it comes a similar binding of the way a person thinks, and consequently acts. An alienated person cannot see others as fellow human beings. They are simply obstacles to the satisfaction of that person's craving for something which assures him that he exists and that he matters. When the power of religion is used to satisfy that craving, religion becomes dangerous and destructive. Bad religion, in its most extreme form, can then justify the physical and psychological cruelty which Dawkins deplores. Bad religion is violent, emotionally and sometimes physically, and finds expression through various kinds of religious fundamentalisms, including atheism itself.

Bad religion also emerges closer to home, in the way ordinary Christians behave towards each other with regard to the issues which divide us, specifically those of sexuality and gender in the context of the life of the Church and ordained ministry. Space does not permit a detailed discussion of the arguments both 'for' and 'against' these two issues but the arguments will go on for as long as Christians resist dealing with the underlying alienation, the defensiveness, which so compromises our life together as a holy people in the fullest sense.

Unbinding the way we think

In Chapter 6 I said that holiness is about being a certain kind of person, one who is able to make choices and order his or her life in such a way as to reflect the purposes of a loving God. We are commanded to love God with our minds, as well as with our hearts. But how is it possible to love with one's mind? Anyone who has been privileged to learn with a good teacher has probably come to understand what this involves. The best teachers are those who allow you to discover things that you perhaps always knew but which until then had lain dormant somewhere in your consciousness. Good teachers allow you to learn with them. They don't simply impart information in order to give the impression that they are especially clever. They are to be found in any learning environment, from nursery school to university, and in any tuition situation, from higher mathematics to passing a driving test or learning to swim. They are people who unbind the intelligence or skill of another person, so they are saviour–liberator figures as well. A good teacher can change a person's life.

Good teachers are creatively intelligent. Their minds are constantly being challenged and resourced from the heart, from their love for those they teach and from their love of their subject and of learning in general, so their teaching mirrors the creative activity of God. In the word 'wisdom' Scripture combines these two aspects of God's active working in our lives. Wisdom is both God's heart thinking and his creative working for his good purposes. 'Wisdom' in the Hebrew Bible is also another word for the 'breath' of God, his *ruah*. In the later Greek texts, it is his *sophia*, the knowledge and intelligence which is of God. There is a close correlation between the dynamic generative force of God's love revealed in Christ and the activity, or working, of his Holy Spirit throughout Scripture and in the life of the Church today. This loving dynamic force unbinds the thinking and creative life of the person who remains connected to God in prayer, and it unbinds attitudes, mindsets and preconceptions in the life of the Christian community. It gives what the psalmist calls 'understanding' (Ps. 119.34).

Heart thinking

'Understanding' is also another word for the Wisdom which is of God. When the psalmist in Psalm 119.34 asks for understanding 'that I may keep your law', he is asking for the kind of understanding which only God can give, the kind which will impart meaning and purpose to his life. Wisdom is 'heart thinking', which allows the intelligence to be informed by God's love and from within a person's own love for God. It ought therefore to become the basis from which Christians begin to look at the causes of alienation in their lives together. Wisdom is the means whereby we recognize and receive God's love. It creates a 'space' in our shared consciousness for receiving the grace we need for healing and reconciliation. Unfortunately, the kind of wisdom I am talking about does not come with a clear set of instructions telling us how to do this. Nor does it rely on information or solve problems in a strategic way. There are probably not many heart thinkers heading up government committees and decision-making bodies.

It is in the Wisdom literature of the Scriptures that we learn about heart thinking, and in the great spiritual writers of the Church; also in the work of poets, writers and playwrights, who make it their job to reveal us to ourselves. Heart thinking, and the wisdom it brings, involve our taking risks by being prepared to go to the limits in the way we think about our faith, by being intellectually and creatively 'edgy'. Edginess and the Wisdom of God belong together because they are only to be found in the border areas, where the holy is often discovered in the violent and even sacrilegious. I was once involved with a production of *Faust* in which we found the holy through exploring evil in all its banality and silliness while keeping hold of the play's dark and deeply disturbing spiritual focus.[4] We, the actors, had to think ourselves into this dark place and perform ideas which took us to the edge of the sacrilegious so that we could bring the audience with us through that darkness into a richer experience of Christ.

Wisdom is about creativity, so it breaks down barriers and moves us on. It draws on the love of God and trusts him, even when that takes us into difficult places. As with the work of artists, directors and playwrights, heart thinking is a two-way intellectual process which involves a readiness to go with the truth as God gives it. Simone Weil, in her book *Waiting on God*, describes every intellectual exercise as a pursuit of the truth, a waiting exercise rather than a search for absolutes and finite answers, 'a special way of waiting upon truth, setting our hearts upon it, yet not allowing ourselves to go out in search of it'.[5]

There is a sense, therefore, in which different ways of apprehending what is true for a community, or according to God's good purpose for it, meet in the same place, a place where we wait on God together. We find our way to God, and to his truth for us now, via different routes, or different 'ways'. The different ways lead to the same truth. They join the 'way' which is Christ and Christ joins us to God, like the roads which lead to a dual carriageway and ultimately to a town or other converging point.

For freedom Christ has set us free

The problem comes when a person or group who are trying to figure out what is really the right way to think or act get thrown off course by fear. They fear that they may have got it all wrong and that God will therefore disown them. They also fear what other Christians will think if they come to the 'wrong' conclusions about any one issue. In this respect, and irrespective of churchmanship, Christians often become very fearful when they are faced with inconsistencies in Scripture as well as in the life and teaching of the Church. When this happens, they no longer know what to think, or what God wishes them to do. In our present divisions we fear the Christians we do not understand, or with whom we cannot fully identify, either because of their sexual orientation or because they are breaking old rules and conventions relating to gender roles and the perceived limitations of these roles in the life of the Church. The more they fear what they do not fully understand, the more self-protective Christians become in their relations with one another.

Where there is fear and lack of trust individuals and groups shore up their self-confidence through violent attitudes and behaviour towards those they do not understand. It is still acceptable in certain circles to make jokes about the Virgin Mary and to mock the idea of religious orders. In others, it is equally acceptable to mock certain kinds of worship songs by parodying the words in such a way as to make the Christians who use them sound ridiculous. I have witnessed both these forms of discourtesy during my time in ministry.

All this suggests that our relationships are deficient in two areas. First, in a loss of confidence about who we really are, that we are a people who have been forgiven and accepted in Christ and, second, in a similar loss of confidence in the freedom we have been given to think through our faith. Christians need to be continually thinking about God as well as loving him. If they do not think about him, they will neither know him nor understand his will and purpose for their lives, so they will find it difficult to go on knowing and loving him in the challenges and inconsistencies of life in the twenty-first century.

This is the 'context' in which we are called to make sense of the religion which binds us to a loving God who we come to know in Jesus. Making sense of the Christian faith is not about proving or disproving what Christians believe, in the way you might prove a scientific theory. This is the mistake which

Richard Dawkins makes. He reduces faith to the sort of belief that is no different from belief in Santa Claus or tooth fairies, as if all people of faith, and Christians in particular, are clinging to a state of infantile delusion.[6] I ceased to believe in Santa Claus on the night I happened to be awake when my stepfather brought in our Christmas stockings but I went on 'believing' because it would have spoiled the magic of Christmas not to do so. This was not faith. It was a deliberately willed childish delusion. Paul tells the Corinthian church that their immature behaviour shows that they are stuck in a childish form of belief, so when it comes to talking about the meaning of salvation in Jesus Christ, he can only feed them milk when by now they should be on solids (1 Cor. 3.2). Faith involves continually reviewing the way we believe, from the earliest stages of our faith journey up to the present moment, so that we can know and love God better.

These two areas, the mind and the heart, or the spirit and the rational, inform one another. When they become separated, we end up lacking the nourishment which makes for a solid faith. The writer of the letter to the Colossians[7] says that Christians should guard against being blown about by the latest intellectual fashion, by which he probably means those ideas derived from a pagan or Gnostic intellectual environment (Col. 2.8, 18). It is easy to interpret this as a general disapproval of worldly thinking. Many Christians equate worldly thinking with a relativism which leads to universalism and a general 'anything goes' approach to Scripture. While this may sometimes happen, a rich and robust faith does require a certain amount of worldly thinking and good teachers to think with. Good teachers keep us from deluding ourselves. They keep us honest in our thinking and they keep our love for God alive. They prevent thinking from deteriorating into a state of cynicism and doubt, in which things can only be true if they are empirically provable.

Faith obliges us to re-examine, in a spirit of 'wondering' and of 'not knowing', the ideas we hold to be true, so that we can dare to ask ourselves if a particular take on a given issue or question is true, in precisely the way we have always thought, for people living now. 'How do you read?' is a question Jesus frequently puts to people when they try to challenge him, or set intellectual traps for him to fall into. In asking it, he invites them to take responsibility for truthful inquiry and for the moral decisions they make, and he invites us to do the same. The freedom for which we have been set free is a freedom of the intellect, as well as of the spirit. We have been given permission to 'read' and think through what God is saying and doing in the Church today so that we can be faithful to him now.

Thinking through our faith

During my time as a university chaplain I was privileged to help a number of people think through their faith. The chaplaincy became a 'safe space', where it was possible to ask questions and work through ideas, or get new ideas, about who Jesus might be for them today and what the Christian religion really meant to them. Following the weekly Eucharist, we held a Bible study when we would try to discern together what Scripture was saying to us now, both personally and as a Christian community. We would have supper together afterwards, so the word of God was embedded in the hospitality of chaplaincy life. The hospitality of the Eucharist informed the conversations which followed. We learned from this that good theological conversations happen when people are intellectually hospitable towards one another. A glass of wine and a sense of humour also help! Practising intellectual hospitality required that everyone began from a position of trust whereby we took it as a given that we were all seeking to know and love the same Lord.

'Do we all love the same Lord?' This was a question we frequently returned to. The intellectual ethos of the chaplaincy was about bringing together knowledge of God with love for God. It was when we allowed knowledge and love to inform each other that we saw God use our common life to his service in the context of the university or workplace. But we had to take risks, so the Bible studies were often deliberately provocative, not for the sake of being controversial, but in order to allow people to broaden their theological horizons and not get stuck in a particular way of interpreting Scripture. It was by moving together in love and in a desire to know God better that we occasionally glimpsed a wider intellectual 'space' in which to grow in holiness as a community.

In his conversations with the religious experts, Jesus addresses the way their thinking has narrowed and become stuck in legalism and in the outward forms of religion. These were things which constrained their growth into real holiness. Jesus also treats the whole person, both in his conversations and in his ministry. When healing the sick, he is as concerned for their hearts and minds, for the inner person, as he is about their physical healing. Sometimes his concern for a person's spiritual health appears to be paramount. He releases the paralysed man who was lowered through the roof by his friends, but he first forgives the man his sins (Mark 2.1–12). He gives him back his freedom in giving him back responsibility for his life, a life which until now has been paralysed by destructive thoughts, thoughts about himself and the past which are known only to Jesus and to the man he is healing.

Something similar happens in Jesus' conversation with the paralysed man at the pool of Bethesda (John 5.2–15). This man blames others for the fact that it is always someone else who gets to the healing pool before him, so he can tell himself that it is someone else's fault that he is still sick. Jesus asks him if he really *wants* to be healed. This is an empowering question but it also brings responsibility. It gives the man back the dignity of his humanity, autonomy over his own person and responsibility for making moral choices. So Jesus not only restores him to physical health, but also gives him the freedom to admit his need for God's forgiveness.

Being an adult in Christ brings freedom and responsibility. The freedom given to Christians is the life and energy of God's Spirit, that same unpredictable and dynamic Spirit which visited the apostles at Pentecost and which Christ described in his conversation with Nicodemus. Christians have a responsibility to work with this freedom and in this Spirit so that they can become channels of God's healing. They can begin doing this right now by being good teachers; by listening and learning with those who are attracted to the faith but prefer to keep a safe distance from churches and Christian gatherings. Listening and learning with others requires that Christians continually rethink their love for God so that they can communicate that love in a more meaningful way.

Churches and Christian gatherings can sometimes come across as being neither meaningful nor free. Instead of communicating God's love in a way which makes sense for people asking questions, they seem to be bound to the thinking which defines or identifies them. 'Tradition', or being 'liberal', or 'biblical', binds them and becomes their religion. It takes over their intellectual and spiritual life, rendering it meaningless for others. As a result, communities end up talking to themselves because their intellectual life has become separated from the freedom and vitality of God's love. Their identity as a 'liberal' or 'biblical' church paralyses their thinking and creates distrust.

The kind of freedom I have been talking about comes with being vulnerable to God's Spirit, who untidies our safe certainties and ways of doing things by blowing them into new shapes and configurations which affect how we think and how we worship, and who makes it possible for us to begin to understand and love other Christians. At the same time, in order to move forward confidently towards other Christians, we have to know where we are coming from, what has shaped our understanding of the Christian faith so far, and what it means to be part of the wider Christian community. Knowing where we come from helps us take responsibility for who we might yet become.

Deep journeying

My own roots lie in the Anglo-Catholic and sacramental wing of the Church but I yearn for unity with those for whom the word of God is paramount, and who have much to teach me. I need them, so I aim to travel with them, and more deeply into God, by learning from them whenever the opportunity arises. I am also a woman priest. I want my ministry to be welcomed and what gifts I have to be deployed to the service of God's Church, but I must seek to understand those who reject what I bring, and I do this by thinking more deeply with them because, whether I like it or not, I am caught up with them in the ongoing movement of God's Wisdom. I am journeying with them into his love and I have been promised with them that nothing will ever separate me from it (Rom. 8.39).

The cross challenges us to hold in God's love those we recoil from, so we have to 'hold' them in our most vulnerable inner space, where our true self is. When Jesus told the disciple John to think of Mary as his own mother, it was an invitation to hold her, to embrace her, and for them both to be drawn into that unique mother and son relationship. So the disciple takes her home with him. Christians are called to take all those who stand at the foot of the cross 'home' with them, not just those we like and agree with. This is what being Christian community is really about.

So, to return to *The God Delusion*, the question which Christians urgently need to address is not whether we cherish delusions about God, but whether our way of living out our faith as a social body is itself delusory. In ceasing to feel the need to be reconciled, in no longer really *wanting* to be healed, we appear deluded because we have effectively ceased to journey towards God. We are stuck in our separate identity zones, facing the wall, like Tonto the dog.

Some people are beginning a deeper journey of exploration because they want to move on from this dead-end situation and experience the real freedom which we have all been promised in Jesus Christ. When they explore other forms of worship or seek to enliven their faith by engaging with other churchmanships, they are not simply crossing the floor to join the opposition. They are responding to a deep attraction to God. They expect to find him as they journey into new or unfamiliar church terrain and as they think, as well as pray, with other Christians.

This kind of journeying is the prophetic task given to all Christians. It signals to the world that thinking through our faith and praying together is not only permissible, but essential. Journeying with one another, and with God's Spirit, connects us more deeply within the love of God. In it, we learn how to make sense of what we believe in a way which reflects that love, so that the world may know and understand God's loving purpose at work in its life.

Questions to reflect on and discuss

- Is religion a good thing?
- Is teaching and learning theology important? How might the way we do theology affect how we treat one another?
- Is it possible to think and pray at the same time?
- What do you think are the signs of a mature faith?
- Has your church or fellowship ever thought it should change? What kind of change is needed and how might this come about?
- What would the Wisdom of God look like in your church or fellowship?

8

That the world may believe

———•◦•———

Anyone who has been bullied knows what it feels like to be an outsider. The worst thing about being the victim of bullying is not that you do not belong, but that you are made to feel you never could belong, that you are basically unlikeable. There is nothing you can do, and nothing you can become, which can make you acceptable, and there is every chance that you will spend the rest of your life trying to qualify for the friendship you never succeeded in winning from the group which ostracized you.

Human beings are made for friendship. This means that every person on earth has the innate capacity for friendship with others. Each has a gift to be deployed in the service of loving relationships with other human beings. But where does this giftedness come from? And why is it that some people seem more gifted than others, or at least have gifts which make them instantly attractive, likeable and accepted? Why is one sister beautiful, talented and clever and the other not?

The reality is, of course, that the beauty and giftedness of the other sister lie hidden. Since no one else has helped her to rejoice in her own giftedness, she lives in a permanent state of doubt about her own goodness and worth, so she will spend her life trying to qualify for friendship, or for belonging, or even for the right to exist. Added to this, is the very real possibility that she and her sister will go their separate ways in life, possibly resenting one another and deeply unhappy in themselves because of the loss of a friendship which might have been, and which it becomes ever more difficult to discover or retrieve as they grow older. There is a permanent vacant space in their emotional lives. In families, as well as in all the social contexts in which human beings seek to make meaning in their lives, there is often a space marked 'vacant'. It is there for the one relationship which is missing, as a yearning for that one person for whom there is no substitute.

I have depicted this rather sad scenario, which I am sure will be familiar to many, because I have witnessed the reverse, a quite different ending to the one I have just described. The two sisters did in fact discover each other's worth. They learned to honour and love each other through a history of shared suffering experienced at the hands of their parents well into adulthood. Along the way, they also found their Christian faith. They met Christ and were found by him. Their friendship with him was forged in their very different life journeys, in the blessings and challenges they were given along the way and in very different church contexts. They came to realize that the empty space within them, which should originally have been filled by loving parents and by a normal sibling relationship, was in fact Christ-shaped, and in allowing his presence to fill it they also found that they were in it together. Their understanding, love and respect for each other grew from having been accepted by Christ, from having been called his friends. So their own friendship became what one would call a graced relationship.

Christians are called to live with one another in this kind of relationship, one in which difference and diversity is sanctified in Christ. They are called to allow that vacant space which is at the heart of their shared existence to be Christ-shaped and to recognize that there is ample room within it for different ways of apprehending and living out the truth, as long as that apprehension of the truth reveals his love at work in their life together. The story of the two sisters suggests that the kind of sibling love which Christians are called to share does not come automatically, or even easily. It is forged in the experience of shared suffering, including the suffering which Christians inflict on one another because they cannot see their own or another's giftedness, or because they cannot live with it in the right way.

The way we live with our giftedness, and rejoice in it together, has a direct effect on the way the gospel comes across to those who may be seeking a deeper understanding of its meaning and who may wish to meet Jesus, perhaps for the first time. Rejoicing together allows Christians to communicate to others in a way which inspires confidence. They sound human and not just 'Christian'. The psalmist compares this kind of rejoicing to 'the dew of Hermon, which falls on the mountains of Zion' (Ps. 133.3), a metaphor for peace, expressing the richness and abundance of God's love shown to us in the good things of life and in reconciliation. The psalm speaks of the kind of reconciliation which effects a sense of belonging between individuals and groups who have been at enmity with one another, a reconciliation which reveals God's presence at work and makes the kingdom of heaven happen in the here and now.

The coming of the kingdom

Not long ago I overheard two small boys discussing heaven. It seemed they were stepbrothers with the same mother but different fathers. They were wondering which one of their dads would be married to their mum when they all met up again in heaven. In the end they decided that the only way to get round the step-parent problem, in relation to heaven, would be for all the people in heaven to be married to each other, in the kind of sublime way only children can imagine.[1]

I think Jesus was suggesting something like this when he spoke about the coming of the kingdom and urged his disciples to pray that God's kingdom would happen on earth in the way

God his Father had wished it. He was not dreaming of a place, or of the ultimate total reform of human nature, but of a way for human beings to live in trust, in the full knowledge of their having been accepted as a single family, the children of his Father. They were to be signs of hope in a world which no longer had the capacity for trust. We tend to pray this bit of the Lord's Prayer in a rather dutiful way, saying the words but not always believing that they could become a reality in the here and now. The coming of the kingdom seems remote and a little naive. The breakdown of trust in those areas of public life which are supposed to underpin and build up a healthy society means that the connection between trust and hope is becoming ever more tenuous. Without trust between people in both the private and the public sphere, and between people and God, life begins to disintegrate, leading to the ultimate disappearance of hope.

We can also view the problem from an inverse perspective. Trust disappears when hope no longer gives it reason to exist. It is like a marriage which is starting to unravel because one or other party is losing interest in the original dream, the hope that was there to begin with, or because the love and the dream have been allowed to run to seed. This undermines trust. The two people no longer believe each other so they become self-protective, unable to give each other the space they need to grow in their humanity. The same applies in the wider context of community, whether it is a faith community or one which is dedicated to a vision for a better world. The vision, or the hope, is kept alive because of that deeper love which all its members share.

Christians love one another in community when they draw continually on Christ, the source of that love, a love which is always adding 'mansions', or rooms, to God's house. So the kingdom of which Jesus speaks is the household of God, whose walls are forever being knocked down and rebuilt so that it can welcome all who come to its doors.

The household of God

Christians are a household comprised of complicated relationships. They need space. Jesus assured his disciples that he was going to prepare a place for them, one which had 'many dwelling-places' (John 14.2). Anyone who has lived in cramped conditions knows the effect which lack of space can have on the household, whether it is two people sharing a flat at university, or a family with never quite enough money to build the much needed extension. Space is a gift. In terms of the Church's life together, it is a gift which Christians need to accept and be prepared to give one another, so that all can experience Christ in the way which is right for them. Without this conceptual space, even the best of intentions will founder and the hopeful love which sparked off a friendship, or shaped the community's vision, will disintegrate by degrees, perhaps even leading to the outright hatred which ends in factions and sectarianism. The Christian community is constantly being brought back to the question of how to prevent the disintegration of love into sectarian hatred.

A friend once described a family conflict in which love momentarily gave way to angry resentment bordering on hatred. She found herself caught as an unwitting observer in the crossfire of the angry exchange. It was, she said, the end of a long day and all were tired when a minor disagreement arose between a mother and daughter. It quickly spiralled out of control and in a matter of seconds became an all-out row in which things which had been left unsaid for far too long were suddenly hurled backwards and forwards between the two women. Throughout the shouting my friend could sense that the mother and daughter were trapped in separate transparent bubbles and could find no way of allowing their love for each other to be felt or heard. Both wanted to end the fight but did not know how. The problem lay partly in the fact that each had expectations and ways of seeing the other which were unrealistic and false. At the same time, each wanted the other to stay in the same room, metaphorically speaking, to return to what she had been, in the belief that this would enable them to speak to each other and be understood.

When my friend told me this story, she said that she was acutely conscious of the absence of grace in that situation. There was a need for something which could set both people free so that they could hear and see each other in the way God saw them. God was needed in that situation but he could not be heard any more than the mother and daughter could hear what the other was really saying. They both wanted what was good, but without grace it was impossible for either of them to understand what this good entailed, still less how God would like to see it come about. In the life of community, allowing what is good to take precedence over personal views and agendas translates as allowing God his own freedom. It involves allowing God to be God in different ways for different people, and in the particularities of circumstances and events, the different life stories, which make us who we are.[2]

The kingdom of which Jesus speaks is one in which people are allowed to become who they are, so that they can enable others to become fully themselves through knowing God's redemptive love in the person of Jesus Christ. So I would like to end this book by imagining how Christians might become effective channels of love to others in ways which answer people's often unspoken need to know and relate to one another and to a loving God.

Being married in friendship

When two people make promises to each other on their wedding day, they do so in the belief that the relationship will last because it is underpinned by friendship. The promises they make testify to their commitment to go on having faith in each other and in all the creative possibilities which their partnership will bring, but they also realize that they will have to work at their friendship if the marriage is to endure and bear fruit in their lives. If they abuse the friendship, the marriage will eventually die. They will not be able to hold on to the trust which enables the shared wisdom we see in couples who have been married for fifty or sixty years. These couples enjoy the kind of deep friendship which mirrors that of Christ for his disciples.[3] They know about how to move on from the conflicts and disagreements which occur in community, in marriage and in everyday family life. A couple who had recently celebrated their diamond wedding anniversary told me that marriage thrives on common sense and on a sense of humour. As a body of people who are married to one another in friendship with Christ, we need the lightness of touch which comes with not taking ourselves too seriously so that we can begin to look for him in another room, somewhere where we least expect to find him, and be surprised and filled with joy as the disciples were when he appeared to them after the resurrection.

If the Church is the kingdom revealed in the shared life of God's people, where would we find Jesus, were he suddenly to appear among us? He would probably not be selected for ordination training and it is unlikely that he would be welcome on diocesan committees, but if he *were* to appear in such contexts he would probably do so in the way he appeared to the disciples in the upper room. He would suddenly be there, making his presence felt in moments of transformation. There would perhaps be an unexpected and quiet consensus, the wisdom of Christ easing a situation of potential deadlock, or quietly resolving a financial or ethical quandary. There might even be a sudden and sanguine realization that there is no real reason for a long-standing committee's continued existence, so that the meeting can finish and allow everyone to go home, greatly relieved to be let off this particular commitment and, as a result, more inclined to work together informally in the future.

The possibility of Christ's sudden appearance is good news for committees. It tells us that the most turgid of meetings can be transformed into something recreative when the proceedings allow for a greater awareness of Christ's risen presence, the kind of awareness that allows the people involved to be human in the way he was human and to experience renewal together in his risen life. The resurrection appearances, and Pentecost itself, are not just one-off events but ongoing dramas revealed in sudden unexpected moments of joy or peace at the heart of our life together.

Being human in Christ is also good news for our life together, our marriage in friendship, because it reminds us that we are 'married' in him and under his lordship. The Church has traditionally described itself as the bride of Christ, its idea of that relationship inspired, on the one hand, by the Song of Songs and, on the other, by passages from Isaiah and Jeremiah relating to the need for shared repentance. Christ and his people are two facets of the same living organic relationship. But what does this lordship signify? The idea of Christ as Lord or King is what gives meaning and significance to the Church, that single body of diverse people who, like the apostles, are called to join with him in making his kingdom happen here and now. He is Lord of his kingdom because his leadership carries the authority of God's love. Because his authority is of divine love, his kingdom is to be desired as the greatest good for the human race in all its diversity, and not just for Christians. But the authority of Christ is exercised in an inverse sense. He is among us as one who serves, so his lordship is the mark of unconditional friendship.

Our marriage to one another in Christ is underpinned by his friendship with us. This means that when we drift apart and cease to relate properly we have to find each other all over again. We do so by travelling along a familiar path to reconciliation and, where necessary, repentance. Repentance, and the reconciliation which comes with it, can be a matter of a smile, a touch, a gracious apology, but it never ignores the fact that there has been a problem and that the problem needs to be addressed. In the graced relationships of Christian community the Spirit of the risen Lord gives opportunities for reconciliation in unexpected conversations, in new ways of understanding a particular truth, in finding commonality in worship or in humour, and in the occasional moment of unexpected consensus in the Church's committees and synodical proceedings.

Committees and procedure – what are we really about?

When those who administer the life of a diocese or parish church do so in recognition of Christ's unique lordship, and his primary commandment to love and forgive, they share with the Lord in the making of his kingdom. The same is true for the global Church, the whole body of Christians. In both contexts, when those who govern and administer ignore dysfunctional relationships, and create all sorts of bureaucratic barriers and terms and conditions for belonging in order to maintain the status quo or simply to get things done, they are not making the kingdom happen in their midst. Such meetings are in fact counterproductive because, having no spiritual substance, they impede ministry and deflect attention from the things which really matter, such as prayer and reconciliation. This becomes a vicious circle in which the cause of the problem, loss of spiritual substance, and the problem itself, become one and the same thing. As a result, official bodies, from synods to PCCs, quickly lose sight of what it is they are really about. They lose sight of the original dream.

I have sat on committees in which meetings lasting a couple of hours have been almost entirely devoted to issues such as fees payable to clergy for taking funerals and the repositioning of parish boundaries. When time and energy are taken up by such things, issues of trust and our need for God never really confront us because in these contexts we do not have to be vulnerable towards one another. This in turn makes the kind of deep listening which enables discernment both irrelevant and impossible. So we are left with a static and sterile situation in which little of real importance for the ongoing life of God's kingdom gets done. This is not to say that structures and formal proceedings are inherently bad or unnecessary, but that they cannot be effective unless they are resourced from within through an awareness of Christ's presence in our midst and by desire for reconciliation. Trust between people breaks down once they cease to hear one another at the deeper level in which they trust Jesus Christ as Lord.

Being Christians together

The good news of the gospel therefore begins at home. It consists in being free enough from our selves to enable us to be vulnerable to others in their humanity, including those who govern and administer the life of the Church. But the gospel is also good news for those who are on the edge of the Church's life, the marginalized, the excluded and the disempowered, as well as for those who resist being labelled or categorized on the basis of churchmanship and presumed positions on doctrine. They are all journeying in faith towards the freedom promised to them in Christ (Rom. 8.2). This makes them disciples of Christ and therefore Christian in the fullest sense, so they need to be able to honour and communicate with other Christians. Once again, it is a matter of breaking through the transparent bubble which prevents them from giving expression to the good they know to be in the other person or group.

The word 'Christian' has a range of meanings and associations. It identifies Christians in the context of those who follow other faiths but it can also serve as a label to separate Christians from one another. Catholics, Anglo-Catholics and liberals often use the word 'Christian' in a pejorative way, to distance themselves from evangelicals. Evangelicals will do the same in reverse, by using it to imply membership, or exclusion, from a particular belief circle known for its 'sound' theology, with all that it implies for those they deem to be 'unsound'.

To be a Christian ought to mean two things. First, that a person has, in the words of the baptismal promises, 'turned to Christ' and, second, that the one who has turned to Christ recognizes that he or she belongs to the wider Christian community, to what we call the Church. The Church is the kingdom: not a separate place, still less a privileged enclave, but that dimension in which Christians show the world that human beings can love one another in Christ. God's kingdom, and therefore the Church, is a particular dimension in which the world experiences the hospitality of God in the person of Jesus through his disciples. The kind of people his disciples are will mark them as his, as Christian, beginning with how they treat one another in their life together. Christians have to come to terms with the fact that their belonging together in Christ makes them not only God's household, but his family. Other Christians are our blood relations because the blood of Christ has broken down the 'wall of hostility' which divides us (Eph. 2.14).

The Church is therefore called to be a reconciled people, a people who have learned to find God in one another, and to honour, love and trust him in the awkward business of making sense of difference and diversity. Christians begin to do this in a spirit of hospitality which they also practise in a radical acceptance of the world as it is. So the Church exists to love and serve God's world, patterning its work on the transforming love and acceptance shown to it by God in Christ.

Transforming love – the work of mission and evangelism

Transforming love is the work of mission and evangelism. Mission and evangelism are two aspects of the same calling, but they do not work in the same way. Not everyone is called to do both, although when one is done properly, it will embody the other, as we saw with the Living Water outreach. Living Water was a prime example of how the good news is embedded in the person who serves Christ in his or her neighbour. It is embedded in the kind of person they are.

The word 'mission' derives from the Latin word *missio*, which is from *mittere*, meaning 'to send out'. Christian mission is God's sending out of his Church to 'make disciples'. It involves evangelism done in a spirit of loving service. It does not involve persuading, cajoling or dragging others around to think the way I do, whether it is about God, the Bible, the Church, or any contentious issue. Taken together, mission and evangelism are about making it possible for people to address their deep need for God and to have that need met in Jesus Christ. In him they experience the truth which frees them to become who they really are and gives meaning and purpose to their lives.

Doing evangelism involves talking about faith. Faith is a gift waiting to be opened or rediscovered in the heart of the person who is listening to the good news being told by the evangelist, so the one doing the evangelizing is often revealing a truth which is already present, though perhaps unrecognized, in that person's consciousness. Evangelists are Christians who, like the apostles Philip and Andrew, bring people to meet Christ, often, but not always, for the first time, either by direct introduction or through spiritual companionship or by catechesis, which is the teaching and explaining of Christian doctrine.

When Philip and Andrew go to Jesus at the time of his last entry to Jerusalem and tell him that two men wish to see him (John 12.21–22), the apostles are bringing these men to meet someone they have heard of and about whom they are curious, who they sense they need to know. Philip and Andrew are facilitators. They are agents of the good news, the news that in Jesus we see a God who loves the world. The apostles are not manipulating the two men, or placing conditions for their belonging to a particular group.[4] They are simply bringing them to meet Jesus, so that if there is to be any kind of conversion, it will only happen as a result of this direct encounter, one which Philip and Andrew must neither interrupt nor interfere with.

The purpose of evangelism is to facilitate such an encounter. Unfortunately, many people are put off meeting Jesus because they sense a covert and self-interested agenda at work among those doing the evangelizing. They feel that they are part of a mission action plan designed to boost church numbers. They may also be overwhelmed by the degree of intensity in the encounter. In other words, they feel they are being manipulated. While those doing the evangelizing might be superficially friendly, if they do not take the time to find areas of commonality, which may have nothing to do with church but through which friendships might grow, their evangelizing will not sound very convincing.

Then there are the kinds of evangelizing exercises which alienate or arouse suspicion by bracketing people according to age or class. A friend told me how when she attended a particular Christian outreach event, she found herself among people who were almost exclusively well educated and affluent. She was immediately put in a group with other people her age. She was 18 at the time and would have liked to share in the reactions and the journeys of a mixed group, especially of some of the older people there. Suddenly the hospitality on offer did not feel quite so genuine. It felt managed and controlled, so my friend never went back. She found other ways and means for developing and deepening her faith at a particularly critical period of her life.

Evangelism is also about good teaching. Again, this must not be forced or come across as indoctrination, something which Christians are often accused of doing. When Philip overhears an Ethiopian trying to figure out a passage from Isaiah (Acts 8.27–39), he is responding to a particular need. He is being reactive rather than proactive. The man needs explanations so that he can understand and relate to what he is reading, so Philip provides them. The explanations allow the Ethiopian to ask his own questions so that he can make sense of the text and understand its truth at a deeper level, not as a set of take-it-or-leave-it propositions, but as something he has always sought but never knew was so close at hand. The explanations release his understanding. They convey the Wisdom of God. They also create a bond of trust, the basis of a friendship which is immediately sealed by baptism into Christ. But the friendship would never have got started if Philip had not been a likeable sort of person, open, honest and real.

The story of Philip and the Ethiopian tells us that effective evangelism does not depend on strategy and method but on being fully human. Christians are fully human when they can accept and listen to one another as the people they are, rather than trying to satisfy some arbitrary criterion of what it means to be Christian, or Anglican, or Catholic and by obliging others to be the same. When Christians give each other permission to be themselves, they inspire confidence in the good news of the gospel. Something new and life transforming then happens between all parties, those listening to the good news and those who communicate it. Everyone is enriched and together they become the Church, the body of Christ. The good news of freedom in Christ has been shared in such a way as to allow all parties to learn from it, both those who are being evangelized and the ones doing the evangelizing. All are able to move forward together into deeper communion and so become in the fullest sense what the nineteenth century theologian F. D. Maurice calls a 'spiritual society'.[5]

The 'conversion experience' now becomes a two-way process. Those receiving the word are like the Ethiopian, they understand and empathize with the language and its meaning and come to know Christ with the help of others. The same thing works in reverse. Those preaching the gospel are given words to say which they themselves needed to hear, but in a new way, so they too are being converted. Everyone in the evangelizing exercise is part of what makes it both good and news, because in listening and questioning they allow it to acquire new meaning.

All this is about making deeper connections. Where the word is exchanged and shared in a climate of trust it yields abundant fruit, like the sower whose seeds fell on good earth (Matt. 13:3–9, 18–23). We prepare the earth by building up our friendships. The kinds of friendships which make for good rich earth are those which may require a little more input, a little more compost, in the form of genuine human affection for another person, and this sometimes requires a little more work. Working at friendship is essential if the good news we are exchanging and bringing to others is to be believable, so in this sense Christians need to re-evangelize themselves before anybody else. They need to be renewed from within, by drawing on God's grace in their dealings with one another, so that they can be ready to receive the new gifts which those who will join them will bring to their common life.

The Spirit of Christ shapes and gives voice to a Church which is continually being renewed from within, in its spiritual life, and from without, in the patterns and configurations of thinking and worship which will emerge when those who are meeting Jesus for the first time join a church or fellowship. The same is true for those who are already Christians but who are exploring a different churchmanship. They will all bring their own contributions and insights to that church's common life.

Some of the most exciting Bible studies and God-orientated conversations in the chaplaincy were instigated and steered by newcomers. When they started to become 'regulars', these people brought with them a particular grace and energy from which we all benefited. They enlivened our intellectual life and at the same time enriched our friendships. They were a proof of the fact that those who are receiving the good news are not simply newcomers to be patronized and 'discipled', but people whom God has already blessed with every good thing. God is already working through them, serving the spiritual needs of the church or fellowship which they are joining, so that together they can go into the world and minister to it as Christ did.

Working all things to the good

This brings us back to mission, or at least to that aspect of mission which involves serving the world and serving one another. Serving the world is not just a matter of doing things. It complements evangelism in being the kind of service which honours people for who they are, so its first task lies in restoring people's full humanity where it has been destroyed by poverty, oppression, injustice and physical or mental illness. In her book *Beyond the Good Samaritan*, Ann Morisy calls this 'community mission'. It has three basic components: confidence that 'Christians have something worth sharing'; 'the "struggle" to humanity'; and 'the mysterious part which those who are poor and marginalized have in the purposes of God.'[6]

Of particular interest is the way Morisy makes a direct connection between community ministry and pastoral care. By pastoral care, she means taking the trouble to find out what people are really going through, what difficulties and challenges life is throwing at them, and placing this knowledge in the context of the wider community, so that the problem of long-term loneliness, for instance, can be seen as a community issue. For Morisy, effective mission is about connecting with someone's real humanity. She describes how the growing number of lonely bereaved people reflects an ageing community. This in turn invites the local church to consider how it might organize ways of addressing loneliness in old age as a community problem, while at the same time caring about the needs and circumstances of particular individuals.[7]

Noticing and caring about human need derives from spending time with God, both alone and in community. The problem which many churches face, where mission is concerned, is that their need for God translates instead into the need to be doing something in order to justify their existence. The result is activity which does not always connect with people's deeper need for the kind of spirituality and pastoral care which will help them make sense of the brokenness in their lives and of a very broken world. A busy or 'successful' church can even be counterproductive in terms of mission. People who are already very busy during the week are put off churches which make still more demands on their time and energy.

Busyness is also bad news for the Church as a whole. Churches and dioceses which are driven by the need to be doing something are almost always committee-driven and as a result very secular. They are like the seeds sown in shallow soil or among thistles. There is little of substance to resource them at a deeper level, so the love needed for building Christian community, and for effective mission, simply gives way to 'mission speak' and to the more pressing demands of mission action plans and other self-justifying activities.[8]

All this suggests that Christians need to step back and look at the bigger picture, which brings me back to what I said at the beginning of this book. We are busy justifying our existence partly because we are fundamentally anxious with regard to one another. This anxiety fosters a competitive spirit among different groups of Christians and across denominations. What is needed, therefore, is the kind of reconciliation which comes with waiting together on the God we all love. This kind of reconciliation takes us to a far deeper place than that afforded by visible or outward unity. Visible unity is essentially the product of a rational decision, taken for any number of reasons, but it does not automatically embody reconciliation.

I hope that what I have said in this book will invite Christians to look beyond visible unity, and certainly beyond uniformity, to the kind of reconciliation which keeps us vulnerable both to God and to one another and so reconciles us at this deeper level. Being reconciled will involve waiting attentively on God, as well as on other Christians and on those who would like to believe in Christianity but are prevented from doing so by our divisions and the way we treat one another.

We can learn a lot about this kind of waiting, and about good service and effective mission, by observing waiters in five-star restaurants. Good waiters hang around in an alert and attentive way. They literally wait. They are vigilant, ready to bring the one thing that is needed before its absence is even noticed. This is something the Church needs to learn in its internal relationships and in the way it approaches its mission task. It needs to be in the world but not of it, able to offer a peace which comes from God and from dealing with conflict and difference from within its life together in him. The two boys who I overheard discussing marriage and heaven were describing the kingdom which Christ asks us to pray for, so they were right, in a sense, about our all being married to one another in the kingdom of heaven. Our task is to begin to live out that marriage now in such a way that the world may believe and come to know Jesus Christ and experience something of heaven by experiencing his peace.

Questions to reflect on and discuss

- Does your church welcome those who think differently about the Bible, or the Church, or about Jesus himself? Or are there implicit, or explicit, terms and conditions for belonging?
- Would Jesus be a 'Christian'?
- How could you attract different Christians to your church or fellowship? What would you be prepared to do, or not do, in order to make them feel welcome?
- Do your meetings or PCCs prioritize spiritual need? Could your meetings be shorter? When was the last time you really laughed together in a meeting? Do you pray together during a meeting? Or only very briefly at the beginning and end?

- What are your real priorities in mission and evangelism? Do they invite people to meet and fall in love with Jesus Christ? Do they reflect his kingdom? Or your church's insecurities and financial priorities?
- What are some of the ways your church could 'wait' on God? How might it then 'wait' on the local community? Or on its own members?

Notes

Introduction

1 In this context I am particularly grateful to William Countryman, whose book *Living on the Border of the Holy: Renewing the Priesthood of All* informed much of my thinking (Morehouse Publishing, Harrisburg, Penn.: 1999).

1 Can't see – won't see

1 *Church Times*, 'Developing the Community Habit', 25 March 2011.
2 Two of the best known are the community on the island of Iona and the Northumbria Community.
3 I go into this in more detail in *Making Sense of God's Love: Atonement and Redemption*, Making Sense of Christianity, SPCK, London: 2011.
4 Phyllis Tickle, *The Great Emergence: How Christianity is Changing and Why*, Baker Books, Grand Rapids, Mich.: 2008, ch. 1.
5 Timothy Radcliffe, *Why Go To Church? The Drama of the Eucharist*, Continuum, London: 2008, p. 60.
6 Radcliffe, *Church*, p. 59.

2 Jesus? Or Christ? On becoming bilingual

1 Martin Buber, *I and Thou*, Ronald Gregor Smith (tr.), 2nd edn, T&T Clark, Edinburgh: 1958, p. 75.
2 This is a very brief encapsulation of the different ways in which groups of Christians think about the redemptive act of God in Jesus Christ and about Scripture. For a wider discussion of these two subjects, see Helen-Ann Hartley's *Making Sense of the Bible*, SPCK, London: 2011, and my *Making Sense of God's Love: Atonement and Redemption*, Making Sense of Christianity, SPCK, London: 2011.
3 These two words derive from earliest Christianity and from the Greek New Testament, the language in which the Gospels were originally written.

3 'But I say to you . . .' Re-missioning the Church

1 Henri Nouwen, *The Return of the Prodigal Son: A Story of Homecoming*, Darton, Longman & Todd, London: 1992, ch. 3.

4 Whose truth is it anyway?

1 These revelations of truth which is already known, James Joyce calls 'epiphanies'. It is the writer's job not to create them, but to reveal them (James Joyce, *Stephen Hero*, New Directions Books, New York: 1944, ch. 25, p. 211).

2 This is also described as *apophaticism*, knowing God in 'nothingness', in emptiness and silence.

3 Gerard J. Hughes, *Fidelity Without Fundamentalism: A Dialogue with Tradition*, Darton, Longman & Todd, London: 2010, ch. 2, 'The Pitfalls of Translation', p. 28.

4 See Chapter 1.

5 Much progress has been made in inter-faith, as well as intra-Christian, dialogue through a semi-formal exercise begun at Cambridge University. See Ben Quash's article on the Scriptural Reasoning exercise, now based at St Ethelburga's Centre for Reconciliation and Peace, <http://stethelburgas.org/>, '"Deep Calls to Deep": Reading Scripture in a Multi-faith Society'; also Luke Bretherton and Andrew Walker (eds), *Remembering our Future: Explorations in Deep Church*, Paternoster, London: 2007, pp. 108ff.

5 Radical hospitality

1 The word 'eucharist' is taken from the Greek *eucharisteo*, which means 'I give thanks'.

2 There was a notable increase in the number of students visiting the chapel in the aftermath of 24/7. Many were coming to the chaplaincy for the first time. Some had been unaware of its existence.

3 An Anglican Ugandan student told me that things happen quite differently in Africa, where people live in more tightly knit communities and are generally less inhibited than we are.

4 Theologians call this 'realized eschatology'.

5 For a concise overview of Calvin's thinking in its wider socio-historical, or denominational, context, see Randall C. Zachman,

'John Calvin', in *The Reformation Theologians*, Carter Lindberg (ed.), Blackwell, London: 2002, pp. 184ff.

6 There are a number of meanings associated with the word *sacrament*. In very general terms, sacraments celebrate, in various ways, God's involvement with humanity and the created world.

7 The lamp had been found near Corinth. Because it bore no sign of ever having been used, the suggestion was that it had been buried quickly by early Christians fleeing persecution. So we were the first to use it, which linked our agape directly to that early fellowship.

8 The Book of Common Prayer (1662), Collect for the Second Sunday in Advent.

6 Reconnecting with holiness

1 The basic instructions given to new campaigners by Christian CND state that 'considerations of morality are more to do with individuals, it being preferred, where the state is concerned, to argue on lines of "value" and what is expedient. Insist that morality has to be a priority for everyone, governments included'.

2 In a letter presented to the Base Commander at Greenham Common Airfield, the Women for Life on Earth wrote, 'We fear for the future of all our children and for the future of the living world which is the basis of all life.' These words were incorporated, almost verbatim, into the treaty signed between the US and the USSR in 1987, which stated that the two nations were 'Conscious that nuclear weapons would have devastating consequences for all mankind', <http://www.greenhamwpc.org.uk/>.

3 The Anglican Covenant is an example of this. For a more detailed discussion of the way in which the Covenant could serve as a framework, or context, for reconciliation, see my *By One Spirit: Reconciliation and Renewal in Anglican Life*, Peter Lang, London: 2009.

4 See <www.studentcross.org.uk>.

5 Some translations lack verse 39, which says, 'The old is good.' What I am saying about moving on does not imply that former ways of doing things are wrong or bad but that we are called to move on if they cease to challenge us spiritually or intellectually.

6 Daniel W. Hardy, *Finding the Church: The Dynamic Truth of Anglicanism*, SCM Press, London: 2001, Part 1, 'The Reality of the Church', ch. 1, 'Worship and the Formation of a Holy People', pp. 13ff.

7 Countryman, *Border of the Holy*.

8 *The Port Talbot Passion*, BBC Wales, directed by Michael Sheen and co-produced by the National Theatre of Wales and Wildworks, 24 April 2011.

7 Reconnecting with Wisdom – thinking and practising the love of God

1 Richard Dawkins, *The God Delusion*, Black Swan Transworld Publishers, London: 2006, Preface to the paperback edition. He also finds this attitude patronizing and initially distances himself from those who imply that people who need religion are, in some respect, intellectually inferior to those who don't. However, much of his own argument in later chapters seems to imply that he agrees with such a view and considers faith to be a fabrication designed to give meaning, purpose and comfort in the face of realities which religious people cannot cope with by themselves, often because they have been failed by their own earlier education. See especially Preface, pp. 20–2.

2 Dawkins, *God Delusion*, Preface, and also ch. 9, 'Childhood, Abuse and the Escape from Religion'.

3 Alister McGrath, with Joanna Collicutt McGrath, *The Dawkins Delusion: Atheist Fundamentalism and the Denial of the Divine*, SPCK, London: 2007, ch. 2, p. 21. The book's front cover also cites Michael Ruse, Professor of Philosophy, Florida State University: '*The God Delusion* makes me embarrassed to be an atheist.'

4 Riding Lights Theatre Company, Summer School 2004.

5 Simone Weil, *Waiting on God*, Essays, 'Reflections on the Right Use of School Studies With a View to the Love of God', Emma Craufurd (tr.), Routledge & Kegan Paul, London: 1951, p. 73.

6 Dawkins, *God Delusion*, Preface.

7 The Pauline authorship of Colossians is now disputed.

8 That the world may believe

1 Perhaps Jesus was hinting at something like this when he said, concerning the woman who had been widowed seven times, that

'in the resurrection they neither marry nor are given in marriage, but are like angels in heaven' (Matt. 22.30).

2 For Karl Barth, this freedom is one of the key aspects of God's sovereignty. For a lucid analysis of how Barth's thinking can inform how we re-imagine the kingdom, see Nigel Biggar, *The Hastening That Waits: Karl Barth's Ethics*, Oxford Studies in Theological Ethics, Clarendon Press, Oxford: 1995.

3 These well-seasoned married couples ought to be the people running marriage preparation courses in our churches and perhaps helping to sort out some of the conflicts involving the wider Christian community.

4 Paul, in his letter to the Galatians, deplored this kind of conditional acceptance. The letter is mainly devoted to resisting the Galatians' demand that new Christians be first circumcised, and thereby declared Jewish, before being baptized.

5 F. D. Maurice, *The Kingdom of Christ*, J. M. Dent, London: 1906. For the purposes of this discussion, Christians become a spiritual society when they allow themselves to be vulnerable to God and to the real challenge of loving and holding other Christians in that love. They are a 'society' or social body when this love regenerates their common life and makes them more human.

6 Ann Morisy, *Beyond the Good Samaritan: Community Ministry and Mission*, Mowbray, New York: 1997, p. 4.

7 Morisy, *Good Samaritan*, ch. 3, 'The Link Between Pastoral Care and Community Ministry'.

8 Martyn Percy's 'Faith in the Free-market: A Cautionary Tale for Anglican Adults' in *Modern Believing: Church and Society*, vol. 52:3, July 2011, is a witty exposition of where this kind of church secularism might ultimately lead.

Further reading

Bretherton, Luke and Walker, Andrew (eds), *Remembering Our Future: Explorations in Deep Church*, Paternoster, London: 2007

Buber, Martin, *I and Thou*, Ronald Gregor Smith (tr.), T&T Clark, Edinburgh: 1937, 2nd edn 1958

Butler, David, *Dying to be One: English Ecumenism – History, Theology and the Future*, SCM Press, London: 1996

Cavanagh, Lorraine, *By One Spirit: Reconciliation and Renewal in Anglican Life*, Peter Lang, London: 2009

Countryman, L. William, *Living on the Border of the Holy: Renewing the Priesthood of All*, Morehouse Publishing, Harrisburg, Penn.: 1999

Drane, John, *Do Christians Know How to be Spiritual? The Rise of New Spirituality and the Mission of the Church*, Darton, Longman & Todd, London: 2005

Fraser, Giles, *Christianity and Violence: Girard, Nietzsche, Anselm and Tutu*, Affirming Catholicism Series, Darton, Longman & Todd, London: 2001

Hardy, Daniel W., *Finding the Church: The Dynamic Truth of Anglicanism*, SCM Press, London: 2001

Herrick, Vanessa and Mann, Ivan, *Face Value: God in the Place of Encounter*, Darton, Longman & Todd, London: 2002

Kimball, Dan, *The Emerging Church: Vintage Christianity for New Generations*, Grand Rapids, Mich.: Zondervan, 2003

McCabe, Herbert, *God, Christ and Us*, Continuum, London: 2003

Morisy, Ann, *Beyond the Good Samaritan: Community Ministry and Mission*, Mowbray, London: 1997

Nouwen, Henri J. M., *The Return of the Prodigal Son: A Story of Homecoming*, Darton, Longman & Todd, London: 1992

Percy, Martyn, *Words, Wonders and Power: Understanding Contemporary Christian Fundamentalism and Revivalism*, London: SPCK, 1996

Radcliffe, Timothy, *Why Go to Church? The Drama of the Eucharist*, Continuum, London: 2008

Tomlinson, Dave, *Re-Enchanting Christianity: Faith in an Emerging Culture*, Canterbury Press, Norwich: 2008

Tutu, Desmond, *God Has a Dream: A Vision of Hope for our Time*, Rider Books, London and Johannesburg: 2005

Weil, Simone, *Waiting on God*, Emma Craufurd (tr.), Routledge & Kegan Paul, London: 1951